PROVERBS

J. Vernon McGee

THOMAS NELSON PUBLISHERS

Nashville

Published in Nashville, Tennessee, by Thomas Nelson, Inc.

Scripture quotations are from the KING JAMES VERSION of the Bible.

Library of Congress Cataloging-in-Publication Data

McGee, J. Vernon (John Vernon), 1904–1988
    [Thru the Bible with J. Vernon McGee]
    Thru the Bible commentary series / J. Vernon McGee.
      p.   cm.
    Reprint. Originally published: Thru the Bible with J. Vernon
McGee. 1975.
    Includes bibliographical references.
    ISBN 0-7852-1021-0 (TR)
    ISBN 0-8407-3271-6 NRM
    1. Bible—Commentaries. I. Title.
BS491.2.M37 1991
220.7′7—dc20
                                         90–41340
                                            CIP

Printed in the United States of America
3 4 5 6 7 8 9 — 99 98 97 96 95

CONTENTS

PROVERBS

PREFACE

The radio broadcasts of the Thru the Bible Radio five-year program were transcribed, edited, and published in single-volume paperbacks to accommodate the radio audience.

There has been a minimal amount of editing for this publication. Therefore, these messages are not the word-for-word recording of the taped messages which went out over the air. The changes were necessary to accommodate a reading audience rather than a listening audience.

These are popular messages, prepared originally for a radio audience. They should not be considered a commentary on the entire Bible in any sense of that term. These messages are devoid of any attempt to present a theological or technical commentary on the Bible. Behind these messages is a great deal of research and study in order to interpret the Bible from a popular rather than from a scholarly (and too-often boring) viewpoint.

We have definitely and deliberately attempted "to put the cookies on the bottom shelf so that the kiddies could get them."

The fact that these messages have been translated into many languages for radio braodcasting and have been received with enthusiasm reveals the need for a simple teaching of the whole Bible for the masses of the world.

Solomon wrote, ". . . of making many books there is no end; and much study is a weariness of the flesh" (Eccl. 12:12). On a sea of books that flood the marketplace, we launch this series of THRU THE BIBLE with the hope that it might draw many to the one Book, *The Bible.*

J. Vernon McGee

The Book of
PROVERBS

INTRODUCTION

The Book of Proverbs is one of the books classified as the poetry of Scripture. Job, Psalms, Proverbs, Ecclesiastes, and Song of Solomon all belong in the same package because they are written as Hebrew poetry.

Solomon is the writer of three of these books of poetry: Proverbs, Ecclesiastes, and Song of Solomon. Proverbs is the book on wisdom. Ecclesiastes is the book on folly. Song of Solomon is the book on love. Love is the happy medium between wisdom and folly. Solomon was an expert on all three subjects! The Word of God says about him: "And he spake three thousand proverbs: and his songs were a thousand and five" (1 Kings 4:32). We have only one of his songs out of 1,005 that he wrote. And, actually, we have very few of his proverbs. "And he spake of trees, from the cedar tree that is in Lebanon even unto the hyssop that springeth out of the wall: he spake also of beasts, and of fowl, and of creeping things, and of fishes. And there came of all people to hear the wisdom of Solomon, from all kings of the earth, which had heard of his wisdom" (1 Kings 4:33–34).

In the Book of Proverbs we read the wisdom of Solomon. A proverb is a saying that conveys a specific truth in a pointed and pithy way. Proverbs are short sentences drawn from long experience. A proverb is a truth that is couched in a form that is easy to remember, a philosophy based on experience, and a rule for conduct. A proverb has been called a sententious sentence, a maxim, an old saying, an old saw, a bromide, an epigram.

The key verse is found in the first chapter: "The fear of the LORD is the beginning of knowledge: but fools despise wisdom and instruction" (Prov. 1:7).

The Orient and the ancient East are the homes of proverbs. Probably Solomon gathered many of them from other sources. He was the editor of them all and the author of some. This means that we have an inspired record of proverbs that are either Solomon's or from other sources, but God has put His stamp upon them, as we shall see.

Dr. Thirtle and other scholars noted that there is a change of pronoun in the book from the second person to the third person. The conclusion of these scholars was that the proverbs which used the second person were taught to Solomon by his teachers, and the proverbs using the third person were composed by Solomon himself.

There is a difference between the Book of Proverbs and proverbs in other writings. The Greeks were great at making proverbs, especially the gnostic poets. I majored in Greek in college, and I took a course that was patterned after the Oxford plan, in that I would read a great deal of Greek and then report to my professor every Monday morning. I read the entire New Testament in Greek while I was in college and then, when I got to seminary, we went over it again. The writings of the gnostic poets were among the writings that I had to read in Greek. They are very clever in the Greek language because so many of them are a play upon Greek words.

There are some characteristics and features of the Book of Proverbs that I think we should note:

1. Proverbs bears no unscientific statement or inaccurate observation. For example, "Keep thy heart with all diligence; for out of it are the issues of life (Prov. 4:23). This is a remarkable statement because it was about 2,700 years later that Harvey found that the blood circulates and that the heart is the pump. In contrast, in an apocryphal book called the Epistle of Barnabas, mention is made of the mythical pheonix, a bird that consumes itself by fire and rises in resurrection. Such a fable does not appear in the Book of Proverbs nor anywhere else in the Bible. It is strange that this is an ancient book containing hundreds of proverbs and not one of them is unscientific today. That in itself ought to alert any thinking person to the fact that the Book of Proverbs is God-inspired.

2. Proverbs is a book on a high moral plane. You simply will not find in its pages the immoral sayings which occur in other writings. Justin Martyr said that Socrates was a Christian before Christ—which, of course, would be an impossibility. And his admirers say that he portrays a high conception of morals. However, Socrates also gave instructions to *harlots* on how to conduct themselves! The best that can be said of him is that he was amoral.

3. The Proverbs do not contradict themselves, while man's proverbs are often in opposition to each other. For example: "Look before you leap" contrasted with "He who hesitates is lost." "A man gets no more than he pays for" contrasted with "The best things in life are free." "Leave well enough alone" has over against it, "Progress never stands still." "A rolling stone gathers no moss" versus "A setting hen does not get fat." The proverbs of man contradict each other because men's ideas differ. But there is no contradiction in the Book of Proverbs because it is inspired by God.

While the Book of Proverbs seems to be a collection of sayings without any particular regard for orderly arrangement, some of us believe that it tells a story, which we will notice as we go along. It is a picture of a young man starting out in life. He gets his first lesson in Proverbs 1:7, which is the key to the book.

The advice that is given in the Book of Proverbs transcends all dispensations. Whether one lives in Old Testament or New Testament times, old Jerusalem or new Jerusalem, its truths are still true. It is a good book for anyone.

Someone may raise this objection: "There is nothing in it about the gospel." Just wait a minute, it is there. The One in this book whose wisdom it is, is none other than the Lord Jesus Christ.

The book is not a hodgepodge of unrelated statements, nor is it a discourse of cabbages and kings. It is a book that makes sense, and it does have an arrangement and an organization. Solomon has something to say about his own teaching: "And moreover, because the preacher was wise, he still taught the people knowledge; yea, he gave good heed, and sought out, and set in order many proverbs" (Eccl. 12:9).

Here is something that will make the Book of Proverbs a thrilling experience for you: There is in Proverbs a thumbnail sketch of every character in the Bible. I am going to suggest a few of them; you will enjoy finding others. Also I think you will find there is a proverb that will fit all your friends and acquaintances—but perhaps you had better not mention to them the proverb that fits some of them! There is a proverb that will fit every one of us, and we can have a good time going through this book.

Dr. A. C. Gaebelein has written this helpful analysis of the literary structure of Proverbs.

The literary form of these Proverbs is mostly in the form of couplets. The two clauses of the couplet are generally related to each other by what has been termed parallelism, according to Hebrew poetry. (Hebrew poetry does not have rhyme or meter as our poetry does. Hebrew poetry consists of parallelism of ideas.) Three kinds of parallelism have been pointed out:

1. *Synonymous Parallelism.* Here the second clause restates what is given in the first clause. (It expresses the same thought in a different way.)

"Judgments are prepared for scorners, and stripes for the back of fools" (Prov. 19:29).

2. *Antithetic (Contrast) Parallelism.* Here a truth, which is stated in the first clause, is made stronger in the second clause by contrats with an opposite truth.

"The light of the righteous rejoiceth, but the lamp of the wicked shall be put out" (Prov. 13:9).

[You can see that the second statement is stating the same truth but from the opposite point of view by way of contrast.]

3. *Synthetic Parallelism.* The second clause develops the thought of the first.

"The terror of a king is as the roaring of a lion; He that provoketh him to anger sinneth against his own life" (Prov. 20:2).

OUTLINE

I. **Wisdom and Folly Contrasted, Chapters 1—9**

II. **Proverbs of Solomon, Chapters 10—24**
(Written and set in order by himself)

III. **Proverbs of Solomon, Chapters 25—29**
(Set in order by men of Hezekiah)

IV. **Oracle of Agur, Unknown Sage, Chapter 30**

V. **Proverbs of a Mother to Lemuel, Chapter 31**

CHAPTER 1

You may not consider the Book of Proverbs a very thrilling story, but it is. I hope we can get in step with the spirit of God in this book, because it has a real message for each one of us. It is particularly slanted to young men—and applies to young women also. It has a special message for youth. This is a day, as every day has been, when young people are looking for answers to the questions of life.

I want you to notice as we get into this book that it is not a haphazard sort of thing. It has a definite message. I know a great many people who feel that we can just reach in and lift out a proverb here and there. I think it is all right to do that, but the point is that when we take it out and look at it, we should also put it back where it belongs and look at it in its context. The diamond belongs in its setting, and in this case the setting is the Book of Proverbs.

Some people are inclined to read the Book of Proverbs very much like the man who said, "I enjoy reading the dictionary, but the stories certainly are short." Maybe you feel that way about Proverbs, but I hope you will see it differently as we study the book.

The proverbs of Solomon the son of David, king of Israel [Prov. 1:1].

This certainly identifies the writer as King Solomon. Evidently Solomon gathered together many proverbs from other sources. He was the editor of all and the author of some. Also we are told that he wrote more proverbs than appear in this book.

The first section of the book is a contrast between wisdom and folly. This includes chapters 1—9.

THE BOY IN THE HOME STARTING OUT IN LIFE

As the boy starts out in life, these are the instructions that God gives
him.

> **To know wisdom and instruction; to perceive the words
> of understanding;**
>
> **To receive the instruction of wisdom, justice, and judg-
> ment, and equity;**
>
> **To give subtilty to the simple, to the young man knowl-
> edge and discretion [Prov. 1:2–4].**

There are ten words used in this section which seem to be
synonymous—and, of course, they are related—but they are not the
same. I would like to take each of these words and put it under the
microscope. We will find that they are not synonyms. Nor are they
piled up to make an impressive beginning. Every word of God is pure,
we are told, so let us look at some of these.

"To know wisdom." What is meant by wisdom? The word *wisdom*
in the Scriptures means "the ability to use knowledge aright." It oc-
curs in this book alone thirty-seven times. It is an important word in
the Bible. It means the right use of knowledge. There are a great many
brilliant people who have knowledge; yet they lack wisdom. They
don't seem to use their knowledge aright.

Let me add something more here. *Wisdom* in the Old Testament
means Jesus Christ for the believer today. "But of him are ye in Christ
Jesus, who of God is made unto us wisdom, and righteousness, and
sanctification, and redemption" (1 Cor. 1:30). Notice that wisdom is
number one. Christ is the wisdom for the believer today. And to know
wisdom is to know Jesus Christ. Paul gave as his ambition: "That I
may know him . . ." (Phil. 3:10). Oh, that the same ambition to know
Christ might grip your soul and my soul today! We need that.

Wisdom, therefore, is Christ. Wisdom is the ability to use our
knowledge aright. To know Christ is not to play the fool; it is to be a

wise man. I saw a bumper sticker the other day which read: "Wise men still seek Him." Friend, you may not be brilliant, but when you receive Christ and come to know Christ, then you have wisdom.

"Instruction." The word *instruction* appears twenty-six times in Proverbs. Sometimes the same Hebrew word is translated by the word *chasten*. Now that is interesting. Let me give an example of this. Proverbs 13:24 says, "He that spareth his rod hateth his son: but he that loveth him chasteneth him betimes." Here, "to chasten" actually means "to give instruction." Therefore, the word *instruction* means you teach by discipline. That is a forgotten truth today. Our contemporary society is certainly out of kilter and out of step with the Word of God. For example, we are told that lawbreakers are put in prison to discipline them and to reform them. That never was the purpose for dealing with criminals according to the Word of God. The purpose there was to judge them, punish them. No other reason was ever given. On the other hand, when you are dealing with a son, you discipline him because that is a part of his instruction. You are to chasten him. You are to teach him by disciplining him. Your purpose is not to punish him. We often hear it said, "That child should be punished!" No, that is not the purpose of turning little Willie across your knee and paddling him. I hope you *do* paddle him. But *why* do you do it? To punish him. To punish him? No, to teach him by discipline. Our purposes are all confused today—we discipline criminals and punish our children. We need to get back to God's purposes. Our schools today are practicing the "new methods" of teaching. What about the old method of teaching by discipline? That is absolutely out. I believe the board of education being applied to the seat of learning is desperately needed—both in the home and in the school.

A man asked a father, "Do you strike your children?" The father answered, "Only in self defense." That's about what it has come to in our day—the children are bringing up the parents! They are disciplining the parents and telling them what they ought to do. I heard recently of a young man who gave his mother and father a lecture on how they should be and what they should do. Yet that young man was under a court order: he had been arrested and was out on bail! I believe the parents needed a lecture, but he wasn't the one to give it. They should have had a lesson on how to discipline their son, and it should have been given to them years earlier.

Instruction is to teach by discipline. God, our heavenly Father, is excellent at teaching in that way. I think I have learned most when He has taken me to the woodshed. Those lessons were very impressive.

"To perceive the words of understanding." Understanding means intelligence. We have another word: discernment. We need to recognize that God expects us to use our intelligence. He expects us to use a great deal of sanctified common sense.

In verse 3 is the word *justice*. Justice is righteousness, and it means "right behavior." I remember a sociology professor in college who used to teach us that right was relative. He used to ask with a smirk, "Well, what is 'right'?" I didn't know the answer then, but now I know that right is what God says is right. It is God who separates the light from the darkness. I can't make the sun come up, and I can't make the sun go down. Only God is running His universe. He makes light; He makes darkness. God is the One who declares what is right, and God declares what is wrong. So you may ask, "Is it right to do this or that?" If God says it is right, it is right. Or you may ask, "Is this wrong?" It is wrong if God says it is wrong. Right and wrong are not relative terms except in the minds of the contemporary average man. The prevailing feeling is that what the average man does becomes the norm; it becomes the standard. That is one of the reasons there is so much dishonesty and gross immorality today. Right and wrong have become relative terms. God says they are not. Just like light and darkness, they are absolutes.

"Judgment." Judgment means that you and I are to make judgments. It is the same as making a decision. The believer comes to crossroads in his life. He must make decisions about which way to go.

Before I came to California, I had a call to a pastorate in the East, and I had a call here to the West Coast. I honestly didn't know which way to go. I had to bring it to the Lord, and I had to test out a few things. After I had made a test, I found I was to come to California, and I thank God for it. We have to make decisions, and we should make them as the children of God.

"Equity." This refers to principle rather than conduct. The child of God is not put under rules, but we are given great principles which should guide us. For example, Romans 14:22 puts down the great principle: ". . . Happy is he that condemneth not himself in that thing which he alloweth." The believer should have enthusiasm for what he does. There is too much Christian conduct which is like walking on eggshells. People say, "I don't know whether I should do this or not." My friend, the principle is that if you cannot enter into it enthusiastically, you ought not to do it at all. What we do, we ought to do with anticipation, excitement, and joy. We should be fully persuaded in our own minds that that is the right course of action. We ought not have a compunction of conscience after we have done it. Happy is the man whose conscience does not condemn him in the things which he allows. If you look back on it and say, "Oh, I wish I hadn't done that," then it was wrong for you to do. In questionable matters about which the Scriptures are silent, this is a great principle that will guide you in your conduct. If you can look back on what you did yesterday and say, "Hallelujah, it was a great day for me," then you know that what you did was right for you to do.

Another principle is that we ought to bear each other's infirmities, rather than simply pleasing ourselves. We should ask ourselves, *Is this thing I am doing an offense to my neighbor or to my brother in Christ?* These are great principles of conduct that should guide the believer.

"Give subtilty to the simple." Being prudent is the meaning of giving subtilty to the simple; it is to act prudently. It means to be wise in what we do. A child of God ought not to act foolishly.

I remember counseling a young couple who went to the mission field. They just shut their eyes to reality, as it were, and went to the mission field. I personally urged them not to go because I could see they were not fitted for it. They came back as casualties. They had actually made shipwrecks of their lives by going to the mission field. They had not been prudent. They had not shown wisdom in their particular circumstances.

Remember that the Lord Jesus said, ". . . be ye therefore wise as serpents, and harmless as doves" (Matt. 10:16).

"To the young man knowledge." Knowledge is information that is useful. I remember a motto on a bulletin board in the science lab of the college which I attended. I have forgotten all the formulas I ever learned in chemistry, but I have never forgotten the motto. It was this: "Next to knowing is knowing where to find out." That is one reason it is good to have the Bible handy and to learn to read it—if you don't know, you surely can know where to find out.

"Discretion." This means thoughtfulness. This is for the young man and young people in general who are thoughtless. I am very frank to say that I was a very thoughtless young man, and I confess that I am still that way. It is always a pleasure to find a thoughtful Christian. I have several wonderful Christian friends here in Southern California. Presently I am getting ready to take a trip to the East, and at this time of year it is a little cool back there. One of these friends came by and brought me a lovely sweater. That was thoughtful. There are many wonderful Christians who are thoughtful, and it is a characteristic all of us ought to have.

The Book of Proverbs will help us see that these wonderful qualities should be incorporated into our lives.

THE CHALLENGE

A wise man will hear, and will increase learning; and a man of understanding shall attain unto wise counsels [Prov. 1:5].

This has been the characteristic of all great men. They never reached the place where they felt that they had learned everything.

I listened to a young man on television the other night who had skyrocketed to fame on rock music. The thing that characterized him was his arrogance. He knew it all. I don't think anyone could tell that young man anything. Proverbs says that a wise man will hear and will increase learning.

"A man of understanding shall attain unto wise counsels." That is actually the challenge of this whole book. Solomon says that if you are smart, you will listen to what is being said in this book. The spirit of

God has a lot of choice things to say in the Book of Proverbs. They are great truths, expressed in short sentences.

To understand a proverb, and the interpretation; the words of the wise, and their dark sayings [Prov. 1:6].

Another proverb carries this same thought: "It is the glory of God to conceal a thing: but the honour of kings is to search out a matter" (Prov. 25:2). I love that. God has given the gospel message clearly to be declared from the housetops. But there is a great deal of truth in the Word of God that is like diamonds. God has not scattered diamonds around on the ground. Jewels and that which is valuable have been hidden away for man to look for and to find. The gold and the diamonds and other precious things must be mined; oil must be drilled. That is the way that God does it. It is the glory of God to conceal a thing.

The Word of God deserves all the study that you can possibly bring to it. The Lord Jesus said, "*Search* the scriptures; for in them ye *think* ye have eternal life . . ." He didn't say you are *not* to search the Scripture. He said *search* the scriptures. You just *think* that you have found eternal life, because you haven't really searched them. You have been reading the Bible, but you haven't found the real message that is there. The real treasure there is *Christ*. "Search the scriptures; for in them ye think ye have eternal life; and they are they which testify of me" (John 5:39). My friend, if you haven't found Christ in the Bible, you simply have not been mining for diamonds—you haven't been digging deep enough. "To understand a proverb, and the interpretation; the words of the wise, and their dark sayings." In other words, God has put these great truths here in His Book. The tragedy of the hour is the ignorance of the Word of God in both pulpit and pew. There needs to be a serious, concentrated study of the Word of God. Somehow there is an idea today that one can read over a passage once and then you have it all. I trust you will see that you cannot get the nuggets out of the Word of God without study.

When I am in Florida I always enjoy going to the home and laboratory of Thomas A. Edison at Fort Myers. There is a museum there now.

The thing that has always amazed me is his search for synthetic rubber. Firestone and Henry Ford had their homes right next to Thomas A. Edison, and you can understand why they were interested in the project and were working with him. There were several hundred test tubes in his lab. Edison was taking everything that was imaginable and testing it to see if he could get synthetic rubber from it. Do you know he found some of it in dandelions, of all things. That would be the last place I would look for synthetic rubber! But that was the test he was making.

As I stood in that laboratory and looked at those hundreds of test tubes and thought of the hours that he and his helpers had spent there, testing this and that and the other thing in order to try to find it, I thought, *My, how little attention is given to the Word of God where one could do some real testing and some real study.* The challenge of the Book of Proverbs to us today is: Dig in! It is the challenge to do serious study. "Study to shew thyself approved unto God, a workman that needeth not to be ashamed, rightly dividing the word of truth" (2 Tim. 2:15).

KEY TO THE BOOK

The fear of the LORD is the beginning of knowledge: but fools despise wisdom and instruction [Prov. 1:7].

There is an interesting contrast here: "The fear of the LORD is the beginning of knowledge: but fools *despise* wisdom and instruction." They do not learn from it.

I heard a little bit of nonsense to illustrate this. A man driving down the highway had a flat tire, so he pulled over to the side of the road. It happened he was parked by an insane asylum, and one of the men from the asylum was on the other side of the fence. He was watching the man as he changed the tire. He didn't say anything but just stood there and watched. As the man took off the wheel of the car, he placed all the nuts that he had taken off into the hubcap. Then he accidentally tilted the hubcap so all the nuts fell out and went down into a sewer, and he couldn't retrieve them. He stood there scratching his head wondering what in the world he was to do. The man behind the fence who had been watching him said, "Why don't you take a nut off each of the other wheels and put them on this wheel? You could drive safely down to the filling station, and there you can buy nuts so that you can fix your wheel." The man looked at him in amazement. "Why didn't I think of that?" he asked. "You are in the institution and I am out, and yet you are the one who thought of it." The onlooker answered. "I may be crazy, but I'm not *stupid!*" Well, this Book of Proverbs is attempting to get you and me out of a position of being *stupid* in life today. I think we shall find it to be a great help to us. This book has quite a bit to say about stupidity, as we shall see.

My son, hear the instruction of thy father, and forsake not the law of thy mother:

For they shall be an ornament of grace unto thy head, and chains about thy neck [Prov. 1:8–9].

That is the important home relationship. There are many who are reading this who have come from homes in which they had a godly father and a godly mother. They were instructed by them, and they have never gotten away from the things taught them in the home. On the other hand, may God have mercy on the parents who are not instructing their little ones in the things of God!

TEMPTATION OUTSIDE THE HOME

My son, if sinners entice thee, consent thou not [Prov. 1:10].

Now the movement is outside the home. When the little fellow goes away, who is the first fellow he meets? Generally that contact will be with a sinner because most of the human race falls into that category—they have not come to Christ. All of us are sinners, but the boy will meet the unredeemed who is really living in sin. So what should his attitude be? "Consent thou not."

You remember that I said you would find a proverb which would fit characters in the Bible. Probably you can also find a proverb to fit every one of your friends—although you may not want to tell them what it is! This is a proverb that fits someone in the Scriptures. Wouldn't you say it describes Joseph when he was taken as a slave down into the land of Egypt and was enticed by Potiphar's wife? He did not consent to her. This proverb is an example of his experience.

> **If they say, Come with us, let us lay wait for blood, let us lurk privily for the innocent without cause:**
>
> **Let us swallow them up alive as the grave; and whole, as those that go down into the pit:**
>
> **We shall find all precious substance, we shall fill our houses with spoil [Prov. 1:11–13].**

The sinner *(unredeemed)* has a plan and a program to get something for nothing. He lives off someone else and makes someone else suffer in order that he might prosper.

> **Cast in thy lot among us; let us all have one purse [Prov. 1:14].**

This is the philosophy of the hour: Let's all live out of the same purse. Generally those who hold this philosophy are doing nothing themselves. They want the working people to share what they have worked for, but they don't have any contribution to make to it at all. That is a false philosophy, but it is one that is common among young people today. It is the thinking and the mood of the present hour. Use all kinds of methods, even crooked methods, to get something for nothing.

After my father was killed in a cotton gin accident when I was fourteen years old, my mother took my sister and me back to Nashville, which was her home. I had to go to work: I couldn't continue in school because we had no finances at all. I got a job at a wholesale hardware company. They sold practically everything, including candy. I worked in the mailing department with several other boys. I want to tell you, they were mean fellows. They had figured out a way to get into a box of candy and take out just one piece and never be detected. Since it was a wholesale place, there were about fifty boxes, and by taking one piece from each box they could fill up several boxes for themselves. I must confess that I cooperated that first day, and then my conscience bothered me that night. I thought, *This is not right. I was stealing.*

The next day I made things right, but I couldn't return the candy because I had already eaten some of it. After that, the management would let me buy a box of six candy bars wholesale. I would sell them a nickel a bar to the men and women who worked there in the office. That last candy bar was my profit because the whole box had cost me twenty-five cents wholesale. That was the way I got my candy. I had to work for it, and I felt that was the best way to do it.

It is so easy for a young man to fall in with a group that is doing shady things. And it is easy to join in with a group who "goof off" at work, as they say today. They do not return a full day's work for a full day's wages. It is so easy to cooperate in that type of thing. That is why the young man is given this advice when he leaves home.

My son, walk not thou in the way with them; refrain thy foot from their path [Prov. 1:15].

This is the kind of *separation* on which the Bible is very clear. "Wherefore come out from among them, and be ye separate, saith the Lord . . ." (2 Cor. 6:17) was referring to idolatry, but it certainly can be applied here. Solomon said, "Get rid of that crooked crowd that you're with."

For their feet run to evil, and make haste to shed blood.

Surely in vain the net is spread in the sight of any bird.

And they lay wait for their own blood; they lurk privily for their own lives [Prov. 1:16–18].

When you get into that type of thing, it will eventually lead you to your own destruction. You will be caught in your own net.

So are the ways of every one that is greedy of gain; which taketh away the life of the owners thereof [Prov. 1:19].

This is the condemnation of the beginning of covetousness. We live in a materialistic age today. I have an article here that is written by a Ph.D., a college professor. He takes the position that colleges must get away from the teaching of crass materialism. Therefore, they must return to religion, as he expresses it. You see, there are a few who are beginning to wake up. Covetousness is the great sin of the hour. That is what the proverb is condemning here.

INVITATION TO THE SCHOOL OF WISDOM

Wisdom crieth without; she uttereth her voice in the streets [Prov. 1:20].

Wisdom is urging the young man to come to school and really learn something. Come to her college.

She crieth in the chief place of concourse, in the openings of the gates: in the city she uttereth her words, saying,

How long, ye simple ones, will ye love simplicity? and the scorners delight in their scorning, and fools hate knowledge? [Prov. 1:21–22].

Simplicity is stupidity. She asks, "How long will you be stupid?" A young man (who is in his twenties now) told me he had been on drugs for three years. He kept repeating, "Oh, how stupid I was, Dr. McGee." Well, here is the question: How long are you going to be stupid? When are you coming to the school of wisdom?

> **Turn you at my reproof: behold, I will pour out my
> spirit unto you, I will make known my words unto you
> [Prov. 1:23].**

Now I will drop down to the end of the chapter:

> **For the turning away of the simple shall slay them, and
> the prosperity of fools shall destroy them [Prov. 1:32].**

It is spiritual suicide to turn from Christ.

> **But whoso hearkeneth unto me shall dwell safely, and
> shall be quiet from fear of evil [Prov. 1:33].**

What an expression this is! I wonder if this could speak of our nation?
We are an affluent society; we measure every man by his bank account, the home he lives in, the car he drives. Are we enjoying the
prosperity of fools? Are we living in a fool's paradise? AMEN

CHAPTER 2

Let me remind you that the Book of Proverbs is not a haphazard book. It tells a story, a connected story. It is the challenge given to a young man that he be a wise young man. He is exhorted to hear, to increase his learning. He is to start learning from his father and his mother in the home; he gets his basic lesson before he enters school. Even after he gets his Ph.D., that basic lesson will still be good for him. It is this: "The fear of the LORD is the beginning of knowledge."

The way to find out about the Lord is through His Word. There are a great many people who say that a person must be very intelligent and have a high I.Q. in order to understand the Word of God. Nothing is further from the truth. God does not say that is essential. However, in this chapter where the young man starts out, it will be made clear that if he is to know the will and Word of God, he will have to study. He can't just dilly-dally around and pick the daisies along the highway of life; he must apply his heart unto wisdom. Therefore, he must study the Word of God.

SOURCE OF TRUE WISDOM

My son, if thou wilt receive my words, and hide my commandments with thee [Prov. 2:1].

"My son"—obviously, this is advice being given to a young man. He started out as a little boy in the home. Now he has grown up enough to go out and face life, and he is given this advice by some wise person. Perhaps this is his first lesson in school—unfortunately he would not learn this in our modern schools.

"Receive my words (sayings)." The sayings of God are to be received. His commandments are to be hidden or stored up. Store them up with your valuables. I know a man who goes to his safety deposit box regularly each week. He goes to count what he has stored there. He loves to go where his wealth is. He has stored up some stocks and bonds, and he just loves to go and look them over. I know a lady who owns precious jewelry. She loves to take it out often and admire it. She enjoys just looking at it. She keeps it stored up. That is the way the Word of God should be stored up, hidden, laid up. "Hide my comandments with thee."

So that thou incline thine ear unto wisdom, and apply thine heart to understanding [Prov. 2:2].

"Incline thine ear"—keep your ear open. Something is to enter the head through the ear gate, but its final destination is the heart. When the Word of God gets into the heart, it brings understanding.

He still is not through with this injunction, this urging, this challenge.

Yea, if thou criest after knowledge, and liftest up thy voice for understanding [Prov. 2:3].

The apostle Peter said it this way: "As newborn babes, desire the sincere milk of the word, that ye may grow thereby" (1 Pet. 2:2). Have you ever watched a little baby when his mamma is fixing the bottle? He wiggles everything he has—his hands, his mouth, and his feet—in anticipation. I tell you, he *desires* the milk in his bottle. The child of God should be that way about the milk of the Word of God. This is one of the things I have noted about the spiritual movement in our day. Where it is present, you see a renewed interest in the Word of God. I notice many young people today carrying notebooks and Bibles, and they take notes on everything. I speak around the country in many places, and I can tell if there is a real moving of the spirit of God. It is evidenced by this desire for the Word of God. "If thou criest after knowledge"—and remember that the fear of the Lord is the beginning of knowledge.

"Liftest up thy voice." If students want to have a protest movement in college, I would like to see this kind of protest movement carried on: "We want understanding!" This, you see, is advice for the young man: "Lift up thy voice for understanding."

If thou seekest her as silver, and searchest for her as for hid treasures [Prov. 2:4].

Out here in the desert of California there are quite a few silver mines. Stories are told about the early days when men came all the way across the country for the silver. Silver was found in the area of Death Valley, and many a man died there while trying to get to the silver. That is why it was named Death Valley. Even after the men got to the silver, they had to make all kinds of sacrifices to market it. That is the way we should go after knowledge, knowledge of the Word of God. Seek her as silver, just as if you were out mining, looking for something very valuable.

Then shalt thou understand the fear of the LORD, and find the knowledge of God [Prov. 2:5].

This is talking about something that is more than devotional reading, I really don't believe in devotional reading, because I know individuals and families who have been doing that kind of reading for years, and they are as ignorant of the Bible as the goat grazing on the hillside. You cannot learn the Word of God by getting in a pious frame of mind and then reading a few verses of Scripture. The way to get it is to lay it up, to incline your ear, to apply your heart, to cry after it, to lift up your voice, to seek it as silver, to search for it as if it were a hidden treasure. When you go at it like that, you will learn something. You will understand what is "the fear of the LORD, and find the knowledge of God."

I used to teach Bible when we had a Bible Institute here in Southern California, and I had several hundred students. It was always amusing to me to hear the very pious students on the morning before an exam say, "Dr. McGee, we're not prepared for the exam today. We had a prayer meeting last night." I would ask them, "What did you pray about?" They would tell how they prayed for China or Africa or some far-off place. I would answer, "You know, the most important thing in the world for you last night was not to pray." They would look at me in amazement—"We're not to pray?" I said, "Right. There is a time to *study*." Then I would show them Proverbs 2 and tell them, "Last night was the time for you to do the digging, the searching it out. There is nothing here about a prayer meeting." They were in school to learn the Word of God. I never excused them from an exam on the pretext that they had a prayer meeting instead of study time.

There were others who had been brought up on devotional reading. They would read a few verses and then put the Bible under their pillows. I used to tell them, "You can't learn the kings of Israel and Judah by sticking your Bible under your pillow and expecting that during the night the knowledge will come up through the duck feathers into your brain! You cannot learn the Word of God that way!"

I remember in seminary we were assigned a certain theology book. It was a boring book—certainly not like a mystery story. We had a difficult test coming up, and one of my classmates complained to the professor, "Doctor, this is the driest book I've ever read!" The professor's answer was, "Then dampen it with a little sweat from your brow."

There is no hocus-pocus way of learning the Word of God. There is no easy, pious way of learning it. There is no substitute for just digging it out. And it doesn't require a high I.Q. Notice the next verse:

For the LORD giveth wisdom: out of his mouth cometh knowledge and understanding [Prov. 2:6].

If you want wisdom, ask Him for it. ". . . Eye hath not seen, nor ear heard, neither have entered into the heart of man, the things which God hath prepared for them that love him." Then how are we to know them? "But God hath revealed them unto us by his Spirit: for the Spirit searcheth all things, yea, the deep things of God" (1 Cor. 2:9–10). They are revealed to us by the Spirit of God. He is here today to be our Teacher. When I was a young Christian, one of the most wonderful things I learned was this truth that the Spirit of God would open up the things of God to me. This is the reason that some folk who don't have a Ph.D. or a Th.D. degree have a knowledge of the Word of God which others do not have.

When I was a young preacher in Nashville, Tennessee, a 6:00 A.M. radio program was made available to the ministers in town. None of the other ministers wanted it, but I was young and single, so I didn't mind getting up at that hour. I tried to teach the Word of God, but nobody seemed to be interested in it except one person. She was a black lady who would pass my church every morning. Sometimes I would be out there changing the bulletin board as she would come by on her way to work. She would say, "Dr. McGee, I heard you this morning," and she would stand and discuss with me those things that had been on the program. She had real spiritual discernment. She told me that she only finished grade school, but I am here to tell you that that wonderful, black Christian lady knew more theology than the average Christian of any church in that city with whom I had come in contact. She knew how to discuss the Word of God. She had a Bible, and the Lord gave her wisdom. I have never seen a Bible more worn than the one she carried. She used it. She read it. And she understood it because she was willing to let the spirit of God be her Teacher. "The LORD giveth wisdom."

Dr. Harry A. Ironside made a statement years ago: "It is to be feared that even among those who hold and value much precious truth, diligent Bible study is on the wane." I am afraid this is still true, although at the time I am writing, there is a renewed interest in Bible study. "For the LORD giveth wisdom: out of his mouth cometh knowledge and understanding." How can we hear Him speaking? As I so often say, the Bible is the Word of God. He speaks to us by means of this Book.

He layeth up sound wisdom for the righteous: he is a buckler to them that walk uprightly.

He keepth the paths of judgment, and preserveth the way of his saints [Prov. 2:7–8].

Many Christians are out in the fog today; they wonder where to turn. It is obvious that the problem is that they are so far from the Word of God. This Book gives us what He is saying. The Word of God is like a foghorn. It "preserveth the way of his saints." That is what He will do, and He will not do it haphazardly. You must come to the Word of God.

Then shalt thou understand righteousness, and judgment, and equity; yea, every good path [Prov. 2:9]

It is sad to see so many men in public office today, guiding the destiny of nations, who are not being guided by the Lord. The Lord *wants* to guide them. Oh, if only they would go to Him for wisdom! For the man who has a deep-down desire to live in the power of the truth revealed in the Word of God, God will be a "buckler." He will be a defense for His own, keeping them safe as they tread the paths of judgment, preserving their way.

Sometimes folk write to me and say, "I see that you hold the truth." I like that, but that is not the really important thing. What is important is that the truth holds me. There is a big difference between those two. We are told that in the last days there will be vain talkers and deceivers. I don't want to be in that category. I don't want to speak with great, swelling words. I don't want to boast of a great knowledge of prophecy or dispensational teaching or ecclesiastical truth or philosophy or psychology. We have too much of that around already. What we need are people who "understand righteousness, and judgment, and equity; yea, every good path."

THE YOUNG MAN'S ENEMIES

When wisdom entereth into thine heart, and knowledge is pleasant unto thy soul;

Discretion shall preserve thee, understanding shall keep thee:

To deliver thee from the way of the evil man, from the man that speaketh froward things [Prov. 2:10–12].

When wisdom entereth into thine heart, and knowledge is pleasant unto thy soul" you won't be deceived so easily. You won't be taken in if you stay close to the Word of God.

> **Who leave the paths of uprightness, to walk in the ways of darkness;**
>
> **Who rejoice to do evil, and delight in the frowardness of the wicked;**
>
> **Whose ways are crooked, and they froward in their paths [Prov. 2:13–15].**

My prayer from the very beginning of my ministry has been: "Lord, don't let me be taken in by evil men!" They are all around us, friend. We are going to learn here in the Book of Proverbs that the child of God has two enemies: the "evil man" and the "strange woman."

As the young man starts out in life he is warned of the evil man. Associating with him is always a danger for a young man. After my father died, when I was sixteen years old, I went to Detroit, Michigan, to work for Cadillac. I got into the wrong crowd in those bootleg days. We would go over into Windsor, Canada, every Saturday night, and I was introduced to a new world. It was with evil men. After a few weeks of that (and I was under conviction day and night), I got homesick and went back home. There a minister explained to me how I could have peace with God and be justified by faith. But I shall never forget the evil man. The young man should beware of him.

Then there is someone else the young man is warned about. She is the "strange woman." A better translation is the *stranger* woman.

> **To deliver thee from the strange woman, even from the stranger which flattereth with her words;**
>
> **Which forsaketh the guide of her youth, and forgetteth the covenant of her God.**
>
> **For her house inclineth unto death, and her paths unto the dead.**
>
> **None that go unto her return again, neither take they hold of the paths of life.**

That thou mayest walk in the way of good men, and keep the paths of the righteous.

For the upright shall dwell in the land, and the perfect shall remain in it.

But the wicked shall be cut off from the earth, and the transgressors shall be rooted out of it [Prov. 2:16–22].

Who is the strange woman? In Israel, God had made a law that no Israelite woman was to play the prostitute. I am confident that if any woman did that, she was automatically put outside the bounds of Israel, and she was classed with sinners—and later with publicans. The stranger was the Gentile who came in. She recognized that there would be a place for her to ply her trade. So the "strange woman" would be a foreigner, the stranger, who came into Israel to practice prostitution. The young man is warned about her. He is told what might happen to him. "None that go unto her return again, neither take they hold of the paths of life." They will lose their health.

An elder in a church back East told me that he almost wrecked his life with just one escapade. He said, "I went out on the town one night with the boys, and that one night I picked up a venereal disease. Back in those days it took years to get rid of the result of that. It almost wrecked my life." God warns against that.

In our contemporary culture when sex without marriage is accepted behavior, we are finding that venereal disease is reaching epidemic proportions. When I was a young fellow, I belonged to an organization whose leader was a very fine doctor. He called in a group of us fellows because he saw that we were doing a great deal of running around. He said he just wanted to have a friendly talk with us. Well, he scared the daylights out of me. People today say that we don't want to frighten our young people. Well, I thank God for what the doctor told us and for the fact that he did scare us. That is exactly what the writer here in Proverbs is doing. He warns the young man about the evil man and the strange woman.

CHAPTER 3

The steps of the young man are now steps of responsibility. He has left the home and has moved out into life, out where he is coming in contact with reality. The advice that is given to him is that his steps need to be ordered according to the Word of God. Oh, how important that is! That is the reason a jeweler I know in Dallas, Texas, gave out the Book of Proverbs to thousands of young men. It contains good advice, wonderful advice.

"Wisdom" here is depicted to us as a woman. However, wisdom is for us personified in the Lord Jesus Christ. "But of him are ye in Christ Jesus, who of God is made unto us wisdom . . ." (1 Cor. 1:30). The young man actually needs Christ.

THE BOY IS TO LISTEN TO GOD'S LAW

My son, forget not my law; but let thine heart keep my commandments [Prov. 3:1].

This also is directed to "My son." We are on Jewish ground here—we need to understand that. Nevertheless, it has a great importance and significance for us today.

"Let thine heart keep my commandments." Isn't that an interesting statement? This is more than simply submitting to duty. I hear so often that it is "our duty" as Christians to do this and to do that. My friend, maybe you won't like for me to say this, but it is not a duty. It is the loving devotion to the will of God. Remember what the psalmist wrote, "Thy word have I hid in mine *heart*, that I might not sin against thee" (Ps. 119:11, italics mine). Also we are told regarding a young priest named Ezra: "For Ezra had prepared his *heart* to seek the law of the LORD, and to do it, and to teach in Israel statutes and judgments" (Ezra 7:10, italics mine). There needs to be that preparation of the heart. Then, remember how the Lord Jesus talked to His own there in the Upper Room. He spoke so intimately, so personally, so wonderfully of things that had never been revealed before. He told those men, ". . . If a man love me, he will keep my words: and my Father will love him, and we will come unto him, and make our abode with him" (John 14:23). My friend, do you love Him? If you do, then He wants to talk to you. Let's not put it on the basis of duty. A man said to me the other day, "I feel that since you are on the radio, it is your duty to say this." Brother, just forget the duty part of it. I love the Lord Jesus, and I really am trying to do what I think He wants me to do. He says for me to give out His Word. He's sowing seed today—that's the picture of Him—and I'm sowing seed under His direction. I do it because I love Him. "If a man love me, he will keep my words."

Peter certainly came to understand this. He denied the Lord, and how terrible that was. After the Resurrection, the Lord prepared a breakfast on the shore of the Sea of Galilee. When Simon Peter came into His presence, did the Lord ask him, "What do you mean by denying Me?" Is that what He said? Oh, no! He asked, ". . . Simon, son of Jonas, lovest thou me? . . . (John 21:17). If you love Him, my friend, it makes life so much brighter and richer and more wonderful.

Let not mercy and truth forsake thee: bind them about thy neck; write them upon the table of thine heart [Prov. 3:3].

"Mercy" is loving-kindness. The law was given by Moses, but grace and truth came by Jesus Christ. What is loving-kindness? It is grace; it is more than kindness. The teacher asked a little girl the difference between kindness and loving-kindness. The little girl answered, "Well, if you go in and ask your mama for a piece of bread with some butter on it, and she gives it to you, that's kindness. But if she puts a little jam on it without your asking her, that is loving-kindness." My friend, God puts a little jam on it for us—loving-kindness and truth, let not these forsake thee: "bind them about thy neck; write them upon the table of thine heart."

So shalt thou find favour and good understanding in the sight of God and man [Prov. 3:4].

How wonderful this is!
Now the next two verses are very familiar.

Trust in the LORD with all thine heart; and lean not unto thine own understanding.

In all thy ways acknowledge him, and he shall direct thy paths [Prov. 3:5–6].

In a service where folk are invited to give their favorite verses, these verses are invariably quoted. I'm sure I have heard them given in a thousand meetings. I sometimes wonder if those who say them realize that they come out of such a rich vein of truth. We need to remember that these verses are directed to the man who diligently studies the Word of God, to the young man who listens to God's law. It is as Paul wrote to Timothy, "Study to shew thyself approved unto God, a workman that needeth not to be ashamed, rightly dividing the word of truth" (2 Tim. 2:15). Having studied the Word of God and knowing something about the loving-kindness, the grace and truth of God—holding on to these things—"trust in Jehovah with all thine heart; and lean not on thine own understanding. In all thy ways acknowledge him, and he shall direct thy paths."

Let's pause and look at that for a moment. This is a very solemn admonition; yet it offers such wonderful assurance of guidance into a way of peace. What a contrast this is to Proverbs 28:26: "He that trusteth in his own heart is a fool . . . ." A man was telling me the other day that he was witnessing to some young folks who are in the drug culture. He told a young man, "God loves you, young man." The fellow answered, "I don't need God to love me. I love *myself*. I don't need to trust in God. I trust in *myself*." I wish the man had given him this verse: "He that trusteth in his own heart is a fool."

On the other hand, it is a wonderful thing to trust in Jehovah with all your heart, to be totally committed to Him. Total commitment to Him is sorely needed in our day.

I find myself coming back to this again and again: "Trust in the Lord with all thine heart." I may be in an airport and learn that the time of my flight has been changed or delayed by stormy weather. I just wasn't built with *wings,* and I have never cared too much for flying. (By the way, I don't expect to have wings in eternity either.) I generally go over to a corner of the airport and say, "Lord, I want to trust You with all my heart. Now just help me to sit down here and rest in You." That's when I need Him. "Trust in Jehovah with all thine heart; and lean not on thine own understanding." I go to the window and look at the sky, and I make a prognostication. But He says to me, "Don't lean on your own understanding. In all thy ways acknowledge Me, and I shall direct thy paths." *He* has led me through life.

I must confess to you that I didn't trust Him like that until I had cancer. I took every day just as it came. Shakespeare, in Act IV of *Julius Caesar,* said: "There is a tide in the affairs of men, which, taken at the flood, leads on to fortune." That was the way I took life. I don't take it that way anymore. Every time I come to a new day, I like to go and look up at the sky and say, "Lord, thank You for bringing me to a new day." It may be a gloomy day or a bright day, whatever the day, I thank Him. "In all thy ways acknowledge him, and he shall direct thy paths." It took me a long time to learn what that meant in *life.*

Remember that the Lord Jesus, in the Sermon on the Mount, said, ". . . if therefore thine eye be single, thy whole body shall be full of light" (Matt. 6:22). That is an amazing thing. If you have committed yourself to God and you are going down a certain path, doing a certain thing, it is amazing how everything else drops into place. Then your whole body is full of light. Your whole *life* is full of light at that time.

Be not wise in thine own eyes: fear the LORD, and depart from evil.

It shall be health to thy navel, and marrow to thy bones [Prov. 3:7–8].

It could be translated this way: "It shall be healing to thy sinew and moistening to thy bones." I think that it will actually improve your health to trust in the Lord. It is wonderful to rest in Him rather than in yourself.

"Fear the LORD, and depart from evil." The apostle Paul advised young Timothy, ". . . Let every one that nameth the name of Christ depart from iniquity" (2 Tim. 2:19). It will get you away from sin, away from those things which corrode not only your spiritual life but your physical life as well.

MATERIAL BLESSINGS HAVE
A SPIRITUAL SIGNIFICANCE

Honour the LORD with thy substance, and with the firstfruits of all thine increase:

So shall thy barns be filled with plenty, and thy presses shall burst out with new wine [Prov. 3:9–10].

This represents total commitment. Remember that when God told Israel about the land He was giving to them, He said, "The land is Mine; I am giving it to you." Israel was to bring a tithe (I think they actually brought three tithes to the Lord). At the very beginning of the harvest they brought the firstfruits. That was to acknowledge that God was the owner of it all. It was an evidence of total commitment.

Don't tell me you are totally committed to the Lord until your pocketbook is committed too. The Lord gave you everything. Some folk may say, "I have worked hard. I earned this." But who gave you the health to work? Who gave you the work to do? Who made it possible for you to make money? My friend, God did all that for you. Acknowledge Him. That is the evidence of total commitment.

Someone may complain that this sounds very mercenary. No, this is real spirituality. May I say that genuine spirituality is not the length of the prayer that you pray; it is the amount on the check that you write. That is the way one can determine spirituality.

I have learned during my years as a pastor that the person who did the most talking was the one who did the least giving. This is always true. The people who want to run the church don't do much for the treasury. You may be sure of that. However, God promises His blessing to those who honor Him with their substance.

THE CHASTENING OF THE LORD

My son, despise not the chastening of the LORD; neither be weary of his correction:

For whom the LORD loveth he correcteth; even as a father the son in whom he delighteth [Prov. 3:11-12].

God is going to chasten you as you go along through life if you are His child. Remember that God does not whip the devil's children, but He certainly does spank His own. That is a good evidence that you belong to Him.

In the Book of Job it says, "Behold, happy is the man whom God correcteth: therefore despise not thou the chastening of the Almighty: For he maketh sore, and bindeth up: he woundeth, and his hands make whole" (Job 5:17-18). Now remember that chastening is not punishing. We have confused punishment with chastisement. The criminal is to be punished; the child is to be corrected. I believe the judges in our land have this thing all mixed up. I have seen a judge take his own little son and slap him across the face when he should have corrected him. Then he turned and let off the criminal whom he should have punished. Criminals are to be punished. Our children are to be chastened—that is, corrected and disciplined. That is what God does for His own children.

HAPPINESS IN FINDING WISDOM

Happy is the man that findeth wisdom, and the man that getteth understanding [Prov. 3:13].

Happy is the man who findeth *Christ*—He is wisdom for us in our day.

> **For the merchandise of it is better than the merchandise**
> **of silver, and the gain thereof than fine gold [Prov. 3:14].**

Now wisdom is portrayed as having a school. The characterization is feminine because she is in contrast to the stranger woman.

> **She is more precious than rubies: and all the things thou**
> **canst desire are not to be compared unto her.**

> **Length of days is in her right hand; and in her left hand**
> **riches and honour [Prov. 3:15–16].**

In the Old Testament God did promise long life for those who served Him.

> **Her ways are ways of pleasantness, and all her paths are**
> **peace.**

> **She is a tree of life to them that lay hold upon her: and**
> **happy is every one that retaineth her [Prov. 3:17–18].**

It requires study and effort and time to grasp the Word of God. The spirit of God does not open the Word of God to lazy minds, but to those who are alert and want to learn and know the will of God and the Word of God. One of the great problems today is that many people are not willing to make the sacrifice to study God's Word. A great deal of laziness is covered with pious jargon and pious platitudes. Many folk have developed a neat little vocabulary that sounds good and covers up a woeful ignorance of the Word of God. In these days there is no excuse for being ignorant of the Word of God. It requires work, it is true, but the ways of wisdom are the ways of pleasantness, and all her paths are peace.

> **The LORD by wisdom hath founded the earth; by under-**
> **standing hath he established the heavens.**

> **By his knowledge the depths are broken up, and the**
> **clouds drop down the dew [Prov. 3:19–20].**

You and I live in a universe that is tremendously orderly. There are a number of folk who work in the space program who are believers. Many of them listen to our program and support it, and we rejoice in that. It is strange to me that everyone who studies the laws of nature and probes into the secrets of the universe is not brought to the realization that we live in a universe that couldn't have just happened. If it did just happen, how and when did it happen? Where is the chicken that hatched out the egg? This universe is so orderly that man can take a rocket, put men in it, send it out through space to the moon, land on the moon and come back. Man thinks he is so smart. But what he has done is to discover the laws of God that keep the entire universe running like a computer. My friend, if this universe just happened by chance, it would not operate so precisely. The reason the space program folk can work that little computer and send the rocket to the right place at the right time is because God has established very precise laws. God by wisdom made them. I do not mean to be irreverent when I say that our God is no dummy. We need to recognize the intelligence of God. I believe He would appreciate it if we showed more intelligence, more knowledge of Him and His ways. This we can do in His school, the Word of God. That is the only place.

My son, let not them depart from thine eyes: keep sound wisdom and discretion [Prov. 3:21].

"Let not them depart from thine eyes"—the word them refers to God's knowledge.

So shall they be life unto thy soul, and grace to thy neck [Prov. 3:22].

You see, life and grace come through this wisdom of studying the Word of God.

Then shalt thou walk in thy way safely, and thy foot shall not stumble.

When thou liest down, thou shalt not be afraid: yea, thou shalt lie down, and thy sleep shall be sweet [Prov. 3:23–24].

Man today has certain fears about life. These fears come to all of us. What is the solution? The Word of God is the answer to all of that. Since we spend most of our time either walking or lying down, the assurance is given that we will walk safely and our sleep shall be sweet. How wonderful it is to discover that the truth of God will hold us—it is not that you and I hold the truth, but the truth will hold us.

Be not afraid of sudden fear, neither of the desolation of the wicked, when it cometh.

For the LORD shall be thy confidence, and shall keep thy foot from being taken [Prov. 3:25–26].

These verses have meant a great deal to me because I have a fear of flying. When I sit there in a plane, I wait for the plane to fall! I think the next minute will be it. So these verses have been a great encouragement and help to me. I take them with me when I travel by plane, and I use that mode of transportation a great deal.

"Be not afraid of sudden fear"—don't be afraid of the next minute. God is taking care of me at the present moment, and He will take care of me in the next moment.

"For the LORD shall be thy confidence, and shall keep thy foot from falling." I say to the Lord, "This morning when I was in bed, before I got up, I didn't really need You as much as I do right now. Here I am, 38,000 feet in the air, and I'm just a little frightened. Now this is the test: give me the confidence, the assurance, that You are going to keep my foot from falling."

Now this is a marvelous proverb that we are coming to—in fact, there are several of them.

Withhold not good from them to whom it is due, when it is in the power of thine hand to do it [Prov. 3:27].

My dad didn't like the organized churches and was opposed to them because of a very bitter experience when he was young. But I always felt he had a desire to be obedient to God. Let me give you an example. When I was a boy, we were riding down a west Texas road in a buggy. A gate had come open and a man's cows had run out. My dad stopped, drove the cows back in, shut the old wire gate, and put the wire over the top to close it. He got back in the buggy and didn't say anything to anyone. He never mentioned it to the man who owned the cows.

> **Say not unto thy neighbour, Go, and come again, and tomorrow I will give; when thou hast it by thee [Prov. 3:28].**

How many people today say to me, "I'm going to support your program. You can count on me—but I do have to wait until my ship comes in." Those people have a bank account and could write a check immediately. I use this as an illustration because I hear it so often. But people use this same excuse in all relations of life. They say to others, "I can't help you right now, but you come back tomorrow"—and they have the money in their pocket! We are told in Romans 13:8: "Owe no man any thing, but to *love* one another . . ." (italics mine). This kind of love reveals whether a man is a child of God or not.

Do you know that when you and I owe money to another person, that money we have is not ours? It belongs to the other man. To use it for our own purposes is actually dishonest. That is what he is saying here.

> **Devise not evil against thy neighbour, seeing he dwelleth securely by thee [Prov. 3:29].**

In relationship to your neighbor, don't do things that would be to your advantage and his disadvantage. And don't try to keep up with the Joneses by undermining the Joneses.

How wonderful it is to have a neighbor say to you, "I'm going to be gone for a few days, will you sort of keep an eye on my place?" That gives you an opportunity to reveal your relationship to God in a very practical way.

> **Strive not with a man without cause, if he have done thee no harm [Prov. 3:30].**

Under the Mosaic Law it was a sin to strive with another without adequate grounds. Under grace we are told, "Dearly beloved, avenge not yourselves, but rather give place unto wrath: for it is written, Vengeance is mine; I will repay, saith the Lord" (Rom. 12:19). We leave the pathway of faith and trust in God when we take matters into our own hands. If we have been treated unjustly, we should turn the matter over to God and let God deal with the situation and with the individual involved.

I have learned over a period of many years as a minister that if someone does harm you, you should go to God about it; let Him know that you have been hurt. Then turn the one who has hurt you over to God. Tell the Lord, "This is your business, You said that You would take care of it." I have watched over a period of years, and I can say that God does deal with such people. These proverbs are wonderful and they are true. They are helpful not only for the young man but for the old man and for women and girls—they apply to the whole human race.

> **Envy thou not the oppressor, and choose none of his ways [Prov. 3:31].**

"The oppressor" is the violent man.

> **For the froward is abomination to the LORD: but his secret is with the righteous [Prov. 3:32].**

There are certain people who are actually an abomination to the Lord. In fact, later on in this book we will find some of the things God *hates;* He mentions them here in Proverbs. We'll be getting to that.

The curse of the LORD is in the house of the wicked: but he blesseth the habitation of the just [Prov. 3:33].

"The wicked" are the lawless. This proverb reminds me of King Ahab. The Lord certainly judged the house of Ahab! This proverb fits him like a glove.

Surely he scorneth the scorners: but he giveth grace unto the lowly [Prov. 3:34].

God seems to hate the scorner, the arrogant, and the conceited person.

The wise shall inherit glory: but shame shall be the promotion of fools [Prov. 3:35].

This fits quite a few people—maybe some that you know.

Through the centuries there are many folk that envy the rich. And many have discovered, as did the psalmist, that God judges the rich.

CHAPTER 4

Although the child is now a young man who has entered the big bad and mad world, he is still counseled to remember the instruction of his father.

> **Hear, ye children, the instruction of a father, and attend to know understanding [Prov. 4:1].**

"Ye children" includes the young and the old, male and female.

> **For I give you good doctrine, forsake ye not my law.**

> **For I was my father's son, tender and only beloved in the sight of my mother [Prov. 4:2–3].**

Solomon wrote this, and he is talking about his own father. Notice that he says, "I was my father's son, tender and only beloved in the sight of my mother." There are those who feel that the father's heart was wrapped up in his boy Solomon. I don't see it like that. In my opinion the historical books reveal that Solomon was not the first choice of his father. This boy, reared in the women's palace, was more or less of a sissy. I think he was a sort of playboy, and David did not have much in common with him. Solomon says, "I am my father's son, but it was my mother who really loved me and taught me." However—

> **He taught me also, and said unto me, Let thine heart retain my words: keep my commandments, and live [Prov. 4:4].**

David probably gave him a great deal of advice. When Solomon was made king, David said to him, "Play the man!" I think he said that because he felt that Solomon was not manly. He said, "Let thine heart retain my words: keep my commandments, and live." David had learned by experience that you had better obey the Lord. Probably David was not as kind in teaching his son as he could have been. I have never felt that David was a success as a father. Unfortunately, that has been true of a great many famous men.

The life of David was something that Solomon could emulate. Perhaps you are saying, *Yes, but look what David did.* Well, David's great sins were committed before Solomon was born, and David had turned from that type of life altogether.

Now Solomon is giving advice to a young man, and he is really laying it on the line.

> **Get wisdom, get understanding: forget it not; neither decline from the words of my mouth.**
>
> **Forsake her not, and she shall preserve thee: love her, and she shall keep thee [Prov. 4:5–6].**

Wisdom is depicted as a lady who keeps a school and sends out her catalog. Remember that there is another woman, the stranger woman, who is also bidding for the interest of the young man. Wisdom is urging him to come to her school so that he might be wise.

Notice that he says that wisdom will "preserve" and "keep" the young man.

The great difference in contemporary educators is pinpointed in this verse. Do they *love* wisdom? In other words, do they *love* the Word of God? It was Pascal who said that human knowledge must be understood to be loved. But divine knowledge must be *loved* to be understood. So if you are going to understand the Word of God, you must bring to it love and a mind that is willing to be taught. Then the spirit of God can open up the great truths to you. How important it is to see this. He says, "*love* her, and she shall keep thee."

> **Wisdom is the principal thing; therefore get wisdom: and with all thy getting get understanding [Prov. 4:7].**

Notice the way he speaks of wisdom. It is not just knowledge; it is not simply having a computer mind. It is wisdom and intelligence to use knowledge properly and to have a love for it. That is something that the souls of men need today.

The reason education is not satisfying is because of the way it is dished out. The most impressive thing here is that we are to get *wisdom*. How important it is.

> **Exalt her, and she shall promote thee: she shall bring thee to honour, when thou dost embrace her.**
>
> **She shall give to thine head an ornament of grace: a crown of glory shall she deliver to thee [Prov. 4:8–9].**

The interesting thing here is that wisdom is to be loved like a woman is loved. When we get to the New Testament, this is changed—Christ has been made unto us wisdom, and we are to love Him.

The real difficulty in our day is not that there are problems in the Bible. The real difficulty is that in man there is not that love and longing for God and for the things of God. When love is present in the heart, this Book will begin to open up, because the spirit of God will become the Teacher.

> **Hear, O my son, and receive my sayings; and the years of thy life shall be many [Prov. 4:10].**

This sounds to me like it is Bathsheba talking to Solomon.

> **I have taught thee in the way of wisdom; I have led thee in right paths.**
>
> **When thou goest, thy steps shall not be straitened; and when thou runnest, thou shalt not stumble.**
>
> **Take fast hold of instruction; let her not go: keep her; for she is thy life [Prov. 4:11–13].**

This is a wonderful call to the young man to seek wisdom. "Take fast hold of instruction"—it is something that should have top priority. It is like saying, "Learn all you can learn."

Enter not into the path of the wicked, and go not in the way of evil men.

Avoid it, pass not by it, turn from it, and pass away [Prov. 4:14–15].

We have noted before that the warning in this book is against the evil man and the stranger woman. That woman is a prostitute, of course. I think we shall see that this also has a spiritual application.

For they sleep not, except they have done mischief; and their sleep is taken away, unless they cause some to fall.

For they eat the bread of wickedness, and drink the wine of violence [Prov. 4:16–17].

This portrays for us how the evil man and the stranger woman live. They can't even sleep unless they have done some evil thing. You read of crimes and say, "I don't see how a man could do a thing like that; I don't see how a woman could live that kind of life. How can they stand to live with themselves?" My friend, these folk couldn't live with themselves if they *didn't* do these wicked things. We do not know how desperate and how deep into sin the human heart can go. There is nothing which the human mind and heart cannot conceive in wickedness. We need to realize that out in this world we are rubbing shoulders with many people who are not always nice. Of course there will be some wonderful people, but we need to be careful of the kind of people we meet.

When I was a pastor in downtown Los Angeles and rode to work on the freeways, I would pray. (When you ride these freeways in Southern California, you do well to pray for your safety, but actually, I prayed about something else.) My prayer would be something like this: "Lord, I'm going to meet new people today. Some of those people

I will be able to help. Some of them would like to hurt me. Help me to be able to tell the difference. Help me to put my arm around the man who needs my help, but help me to avoid the man who would put a knife in my back." I think it is important that we recognize the kind of world in which we live.

I have learned that there are certain men who will become true friends, bosom friends, and I thank God for them. It is men like that who made my radio ministry possible. Then there have been men who have tried to destroy it—yet they profess to be Christians. It is difficult to understand their thinking. The human heart is not to be trusted. We need to be very careful; we need to have discernment as we meet mankind in our daily walk.

> **But the path of the just is as the shining light, that shineth more and more unto the perfect day [Prov. 4:18].**

You will meet wonderful saints like this. Then notice the contrast:

> **The way of the wicked is as darkness: they know not at what they stumble [Prov. 4:19].**

There are two ways that are set in contrast. One way is the way in which the righteous go. It is described as a "shining light, that shineth more and more unto the perfect day." There is another way, the way the lawless go. It is a way of darkness. It reminds us of the broad way that our Lord described, which I believe has been misunderstood.

I can remember when I was a boy that we would be taught about the broad way and the narrow way. Now if they had asked me which way I wanted to go, I would have said immediately, "I think you could have a lot more fun on the broad way." Unfortunately, I think that is the impression most often given. However, that is not accurate at all. The picture is altogether different.

The broad way is a wide one today. That is where the mob is. The crowd is having a "vanity fair" down that way all the time. The carnival is going on. (By the way, that word *carnival* comes from the word *carnal,* which has to do with the flesh.) Down there is the place where they indulge the flesh, and they call it the way of liberty. We hear today that we are living in a new age in which we can do as we please. That is certainly a broad way—that is, at the entrance. But notice that this broad way gets narrower and narrower and narrower. The way of the lawless is the dark way. "The way of the wicked is as darkness." There are the bright lights at the entrance, but down a little farther there are no lights. The people don't even know what they are stumbling over. That is the broad way that the Lord Jesus described. It is just like going in at the big end of a funnel and then finding that it gets narrower and narrower until finally it ends in destruction.

In contrast, the narrow way is very narrow at the entrance. The Lord Jesus said, ". . . I am *the* way . . ." (John 14:6, italics mine). It is so narrow that it is limited to one Person: Christ. No one can come to the Father but through Him. You just can't find a way any narrower than that. Peter said, "Neither is there salvation in any other: for there is none other name under heaven given among men, whereby we must be saved" (Acts 4:12). Jesus said, "I am the door: by me if any man enter in, he shall be saved, and shall go in and out, and find pasture" (John 10:9). The entrance is narrow, but after the entrance the way gets wider and wider, leading to an abundant life here and on into the light of heaven itself. My friend, we need to enter into the narrow end of the funnel, and that end is labeled, *The Lord Jesus Christ.*

That is exactly the picture we get from our verses here in Proverbs. There are two ways. There is the path of the just, and there is the way of the wicked. We will hear more of this in this book. The broad way is described in chapter 16: "There is a way that seemeth right unto a man, but the end thereof are the ways of death" (Prov. 16:25).

My son, attend to my words; incline thine ear unto my sayings.

Let them not depart from thine eyes; keep them in the midst of thine heart.

For they are life unto those that find them, and health to all their flesh [Prov. 4:20–22].

The psalmist said this about the Word: "Thy *word* have I hid in mine heart, that I might not sin against thee" (Ps. 119:11, italics mine). God's *words* are the words of life. It has been said of the writings of a great man of the past that if his words were cut, they would bleed. This can truly be said of the words of God. They are living words—if you cut them, they will bleed. "For they are life unto those that find them." They will bring life and light to you. They bring instruction and direction and joy. All this comes through the Word of God.

Now here is one of the great verses in the Book of Proverbs:

> **Keep thy heart with all diligence; for out of it are the issues of life [Prov. 4:23].**

Another translation of this verse is: "Keep thy heart above all keeping"—with all diligence. This is the most important thing to watch over. "For out of it are the issues of life." The life of the flesh is in the blood, and it is the heart that pumps that blood. William Harvey back in the seventeenth century discovered the circulation of the blood which revolutionized medical science. Yet here in Proverbs which was written about 2,700 years earlier, there is a recognition of the importance of the heart for the maintenance of life. And the heart symbolizes the center of one's innermost being. The Lord Jesus said that it isn't what goes into a man that defiles him, but what comes out of a man. "For out of the heart proceed evil thoughts, murders, adulteries, fornications, thefts, false witness, blasphemies" (Matt. 15:19). Some of the meanest things in the world come out of the human heart. The heart is the seat of the total personality. If you want to know how important the heart is, get your concordance and look up all the references to the heart that are in the Bible. We are to keep our hearts with all diligence. What we hear is important. What we study is important. What we see is important. We should recognize that out of that heart will come all of the great issues of our lives.

Let's not miss the fact that the Book of Proverbs, written long before Harvey made the discovery of the circulation of blood, makes a statement about the heart that centuries later science demonstrated to be true. In the Book of Proverbs (and this can be said of the entire Bible) you will find no unscientific or inaccurate observation.

**Put away from thee a froward mouth, and perverse lips
put far from thee [Prov. 4:24].**

The issues of life will proceed from the *heart*, but it is the *mouth* and
the *lips* that will do the speaking. Someone has put it like this: "What
is in the well of the heart will come up through the bucket of the
mouth." How true it is that sooner or later the mouth will reveal what
is in your heart.

Our mouths give us away. Mrs. McGee and I were having lunch in
a little town in the Northwest and were talking to each other. We noticed that the waitress seemed very much interested and pretty soon
she interrupted us. "Aren't you Dr. McGee?" I answered, "Yes, how
did you know me?" She said, "I've never seen you before, but I listen
to you on the radio." Later my wife told me, "You had better be very
careful what you say. You are recognized by people when you have no
idea that you are being recognized." How true that is, but the care has
to begin with the heart. What is in the well of the heart will come up
through the bucket of the mouth. Our mouths will give away what is
being harbored in our hearts.

**Let thine eyes look right on, and let thine eyelids look
straight before thee.**

**Ponder the path of thy feet, and let all thy ways be estab-
lished.**

**Turn not to the right hand nor to the left: remove thy foot
from evil [Prov. 4:25–27].**

Oh, how careful a young man needs to be! A man told me the other
day that he ruined his whole life by being arrested when he was a
young man. He has a record against him, and that record has con-
fronted him again and again down through the years. In this day
when the use of drugs and liquor is so prevalent, especially among
young folk, how careful he should be. How tragic it is to see multitudes of youngsters who are destroying themselves because they do
not "ponder the path" of their feet.

CHAPTER 5

R ead this chapter carefully and you will find that the young man is counseled to live a pure life for the sake of his home. This is the kind of sex education that God gives. I like this education from God better than some of the things that I am hearing today, even in Christian services. God is saying that a pure life should be led for the sake of the home later on. A lot of the problems in the homes today don't begin there. They began way back in the premarital sex life of the individual.

GOD'S SEX EDUCATION

My son, attend unto my wisdom, and bow thine ear to my understanding:

That thou mayest regard discretion, and that thy lips may keep knowledge [Prov. 5:1–2].

"My son." This is addressed to the young man again. This is wisdom bidding the young man to come to her school to learn of her. In the previous chapter the warning was against the evil man. In this chapter the warning is against the "strange woman," literally, the stranger woman, because the woman was a stranger, one who came from outside Israel. She was generally a Gentile, and she was a prostitute. No Israelite woman was to become a prostitute. According to the law a prostitute was to be stoned. However, as Israel got farther from God, they also sank into more and more immorality. Thus it happened that some of the Israelites did become prostitutes as is indicated in Proverbs 2:17, "Which forsaketh the guide of her youth, and forgetteth the covenant of her God." In that case the woman is still considered a stranger, a foreigner, because she is a stranger as far as her relationship to God is concerned.

For the lips of a strange woman drop as an honeycomb, and her mouth is smoother than oil:

But her end is bitter as wormwood, sharp as a two-edged sword.

Her feet go down to death; her steps take hold on hell.

Lest thou shouldest ponder the path of life, her ways are moveable, that thou canst not know them [Prov. 5:3–6].

There was an infamous gangster in the penitentiary in Atlanta. One of the officers there told me that this man had contracted syphillis, which had not been cured and went on to cause paresis and eventually insanity. That man was a blubbering idiot before he died. The officer told me this: "This man was responsible for the ruin of many a girl. But it is interesting that he didn't get by with that sort of thing. Some girl along the route got even with him." God's Word here is warning against that kind of thing.

Hear me now therefore, O ye children, and depart not from the words of my mouth.

Remove thy way far from her, and come not nigh the door of her house:

Lest thou give thine honour unto others, and thy years unto the cruel:

Lest strangers be filled with thy wealth; and thy labours be in the house of a stranger;

And thou mourn at the last, when thy flesh and thy body are consumed [Prov. 5:7–11].

What a warning is given here to this young man. This gives a true picture of the end result of venereal disease. At last there is a mourning when the flesh and the body are consumed. Here in California venereal disease has reached epidemic proportions.

And say, How have I hated instruction, and my heart despised reproof;

And have not obeyed the voice of my teachers, nor inclined mine ear to them that instructed me!

I was almost in all evil in the midst of the congregation and assembly [Prov. 5:12–14].

Remember that God is not mocked. What you sow is what you shall reap. God describes here what will be the end result of such a life. I believe that our society is already reaping what it has been sowing. The gross immorality in our land stems from the lack of instruction in the Word of God.

Now God tells about the relationship that should exist between husband and wife. Here we see marriage brought to a very high plane.

THE HOLINESS OF MARRIAGE

Drink waters out of thine own cistern, and running waters out of thine own well.

Let thy fountains be dispersed abroad, and rivers of waters in the streets.

Let them be only thine own, and not strangers' with thee [Prov. 5:15–17].

In other words, your offspring should be from your wife, not from a stranger.

Let thy fountain be blessed: and rejoice with the wife of thy youth.

Let her be as the loving hind and pleasant roe; let her breasts satisfy thee at all times; and be thou ravished always with her love [Prov. 5:18–19].

These verses describe love in marriage, and the Word of God makes it very clear that physical love and sexual love in marriage are to be sanctified and brought to a very high level. There was a time when speaking of these things was taboo. They were not mentioned as though they were immoral or some sort of a dirty thing even among married folk. Do you notice how God describes physical love in marriage? God lifts it to the very highest plane. Remember that marriage was designed by God Himself and was given to the human family for the welfare and good of mankind. A part of the immorality of our day is the attempt to get rid of marriage.

For the child of God the Christian home is a picture of the relationship between Christ and the church. You just cannot have a relationship higher or holier than that. That is why it is alarming to see that even Christian couples in the church are breaking up. This hasn't happened in only one or two cases but it is happening many, many times. This ought to cause the church to get down on its knees before God and find out what is wrong. It is an indication that the Word of God is not getting through to people. It is not influencing and swaying the lives of those members of the church.

"Marriage is honourable in all, and the bed undefiled: but whoremongers and adulterers God will judge" (Heb. 13:4). God calls marriage a wonderful relationship. It is high and holy and not to be treated as something that is unclean. But notice the other side of the picture: "but whoremongers and adulterers God will judge."

When I was the pastor of a certain church, a man of the congregation came to me and announced he was leaving his wife and son and was going to run off with another woman. They were all church members—whether or not they were Christians only God knows. I was a young preacher at that time, and I really laid it on the line to him. He rose in indignation and said, "Are you trying to rob me of my salvation?" I answered, "Brother, if you have salvation, I am not trying to rob you of it. But I do want to say this to you, and I want you to remember it: If you are not God's child, you are acting according to the way the devil's children act. If you happen to be a child of God, one of these days God will take you to His woodshed and He will whip you within an inch of your life. I am not sure but that He may even take your life." The fellow just sneered, and he went ahead and married the other woman. The years have gone by, and those two are the loneliest, saddest, most frustrated, most unlovely people I know. I am confident they would both say, "If only I could go back and do it over."

Peter admonishes husbands to dwell with their wives according to knowledge ". . . and as being heirs together of the grace of life; that your prayers be not hindered" (1 Pet. 3:7). This is a real test. When a husband and wife are so living before each other that they have joy and confidence and can kneel together and pray together and love together, that home represents the relationship of Christ and the church. I want to tell you, my friend, that God can and will bless such a home. Oh, how important that is!

> **And why wilt thou, my son, be ravished with a strange woman, and embrace the bosom of a stranger?**
>
> **For the ways of man are before the eyes of the Lord, and he pondereth all his goings [Prov. 5:20–21].**

This is an interesting verse. "The ways of man are before the eyes of the Lord, and he pondereth all his goings." We need to recognize that God is seeing us all the time. God is always watching us.

A man was put in a foursome for golf with three of us who were preachers. He was glad to get away from us when he found out who we were. He had ripped out an oath, and after he learned that we were preachers, he began to apologize. I said to him, "Brother, don't pay any attention to us. We are just three men like you are. But you are speaking that way before God all the time. I don't care whether you are on the golf course or in a bar or where you are, you are saying these things before God." The ways of man are before the eyes of Jehovah and God ponders—He wonders why we act and say what we do. I think that God must get really puzzled by some of the things we do and say.

> **His own iniquities shall take the wicked himself, and he shall be holden with the cords of his sins.**

He shall die without instruction; and in the greatness of his folly he shall go astray [Prov. 5:22–23].

God says that there is a day coming, a day of accountability, a day of retribution. A payday is on the way. Man thinks he is getting by with sin. God says that no one is getting by with a thing. Man's own iniquities shall take him, and he will be held with the cords of his sins.

CHAPTER 6

This chapter covers many different subjects. It starts with some advice that is good for the business world today, for Christians or non-Christians. These are simply some good business principles. You see, God has given a lot of good advice for all mankind, the saved as well as the unsaved.

GOOD BUSINESS PRINCIPLES

My son, if thou be surety for thy friend, if thou hast stricken thy hand with a stranger,

Thou art snared with the words of thy mouth, thou art taken with the words of thy mouth [Prov. 6:1–2].

He mentions two things which are good advice any time Beware of signing a friend's note. And never become a partner with a stranger. The unsaved man can follow this advice in his business, and it will be helpful to him.

The second verse would indicate that the fellow has been boasting. Apparently one of the reasons a man will co-sign a note with another man is that he wants to be the big shot. He wants to appear outstanding in the financial realm. We are to beware of that.

Do this now, my son, and deliver thyself, when thou art come into the hand of thy friend; go, humble thyself, and make sure thy friend [Prov. 6:3].

Don't be afraid to go to him and get things straightened out. Be sure that you hold on to your friends, and be sure that you beware of your enemies. That is exactly what he is saying here and will repeat it in other places.

Give not sleep to thine eyes, nor slumber to thine eyelids.

Deliver thyself as a roe from the hand of the hunter, and as a bird from the hand of the fowler [Prov. 6:4–5].

Don't sleep on it; get the thing straightened out. You are just like a bird caught in a trap if you have signed a note. That is the warning.

Now he will present the positive side. Not only should one be prudent in what he does in his business and prudent in what he says in the business world, but he is also to learn something from the ants.

Go to the ant, thou sluggard; consider her ways, and be wise:

Which having no guide, overseer, or ruler,

Provideth her meat in the summer, and gathereth her food in the harvest [Prov. 6:6–8].

The little ant is quite a teacher. Aunt Ant can reveal great truths to us. One truth is that she is as diligent in business as anyone possibly can be. This is something that the child of God can learn from the little ant. The ant is busy doing what is the most important thing in her life—she is getting food for the winter, caring for the future, and she is busy about it.

I think one of the great sins among Christians today is laziness, and many of the lazy ones can be found in full-time Christian service. All of us need to ask ourselves what we do with our spare time. Do we read the Word of God? Do we study the Word of God? I think that laziness is one of the curses of the ministry today. A young man came to me and said, "I feel like I'm through as a preacher. I've been a pastor here at this place for three years, and I have run out of sermons. I feel like a dried-up well." Of course, then he became very pious, "I've spent a lot of time in prayer and meditation." Well, I asked him, "How much time do you spend in the Word of God? How much time do you spend studying it?" I couldn't get a very definite answer from him, but he inferred that he spent less than *an hour a week* in the study of the Bible! He was a great promoter, always out doing something while the important business remained undone. I told him, "Unless you change your ways, you ought to get out of the ministry. It is a disgrace to go to the pulpit on a Sunday morning unprepared. You should have something to say from the Word of God." The ant has a lesson for that boy. "Go to the ant, thou sluggard; consider her ways, and be wise."

> **How long wilt thou sleep, O sluggard? when wilt thou arise out of thy sleep?**
>
> **Yet a little sleep, a little slumber, a little folding of the hands to sleep:**
>
> **So shall thy poverty come as one that travelleth, and thy want as an armed man [Prov. 6:9–11].**

THE WICKED MAN

We come now to a description of a wicked man, a son of Belial.

> **A naughty person, a wicked man, walketh with a froward mouth.**
>
> **He winketh with his eyes, he speaketh with his feet, he teacheth with his fingers [Prov. 6:12–13].**

Have you ever noticed this in a person? Everything he does and every gesture he makes is suggestive. Everything he says has a filthy connotation. There are Christians who are borderline cases in this respect.

I knew a preacher like that, and I got away from him years ago. I have known some laymen who are the same way. Everything they said had a double meaning. I know of a so-called Christian group of folk who, at their meetings, tell jokes with a double meaning. There is always that little suggestive thing in them. This is something that God is speaking against.

Frowardness is in his heart, he deviseth mischief continually; he soweth discord.

Therefore shall his calamity come suddenly; suddenly shall he be broken without remedy [Prov. 6:14–15].

"Frowardness" is perverseness. Notice that he "soweth" or casts forth discord. Here is a person who is supposed to be a child of God, and yet every movement of his body is suggestive.

In my office I have a picture of a man who has meant a great deal to me. He was not a great preacher, but he was a great man of God. I have spent many hours with that man in the past. He always reminds me of the pureness of speech. Never have I heard him say anything that was suggestive or that had one bit of smut in it. His life was just as clear and clean as the noonday sun. That is the type of men we need today. We don't need more of the bright young fellows with the latest thing in haberdashery and the latest haircut. You see them eyeing the girls even though they are married. Their wives cannot be quite sure about them. But we say, "My, they have good personalities!"

May I say something to you, and I am going to say it very clearly. We are loaded with folk in Christian service today, and we are getting nowhere. Do you know why not? Because God is not mocked. "Be not deceived; God is not mocked: for whatsoever a man soweth, that shall he also reap. For he that soweth to his flesh shall of the flesh reap corruption; but he that soweth to the Spirit shall of the Spirit reap life everlasting" (Gal. 6:7–8). God is not fooled. Our God demands a holy life. Do you know why? Because He is holy. He is that kind of God. And that is the kind of person God is going to be interested in and bless. Oh, we need to recognize that we are dealing with a holy God! I have a wonderful preacher friend who is in what is known as the holiness movement because the emphasis is on holiness of life. I said to him one day, "The criticism I have of you folk is that you have lost your holiness, and you are the ones who should be bearing down on that for the benefit of us who have gotten very far from God." My, what an emphasis is needed on holy living among God's people today!

SEVEN THINGS GOD HATES

It is unbelievable to some folk that God could hate. They consider Him as only a God of love. The reason they have this kind of reaction is the result of following a deductive reasoning based on the syllogistic method of reasoning. The major premise is that God is love. That is true. The minor premise is that love is the opposite of hate, and that is also true. Then the conclusion they draw is that God cannot hate anything, but that is not true. God is love, but He hates evil.

We can see this same thing in our human relationships. You love your little child, but you hate the fever that is racking his little body. You love your child, but you hate the mad dog with the frothing mouth that comes into your yard and attempts to bite your little child. If you love your child, you will hate the mad dog. As long as there is a world of contrasts, a world in which sin has entered, we will love the right and hate the wrong. Or, on the other hand, if you love sin, then you will hate righteousness.

The Word of God tells us to love the good and hate the evil. When we get to the Book of Ecclesiastes, we will find that it says that there is "A time to love, and a time to hate . . ." (Eccl. 3:8).

Now we find that there are seven things God hates. This is His list:

> **These six things doth the LORD hate: yea, seven are an abomination unto him:**
>
> **A proud look, a lying tongue, and hands that shed innocent blood,**
>
> **An heart that deviseth wicked imaginations, feet that be swift in running to mischief,**
>
> **A false witness that speaketh lies, and he that soweth discord among brethren [Prov. 6:16–19].**

God definitely says that He hates these things, and we ought to put them on our "hate list" also. This isn't the first time God has stated that He hates something. If you will turn back to Deuteronomy, you will read, "Neither shalt thou set thee up any image; which the Lord thy God hateth" (Deut. 16:22). God hates any kind of idol or anything that would take His place in our hearts. God's hate is mentioned again in Psalm 45:7, the great millennial psalm: "Thou lovest righteousness, and hatest wickedness . . . ." One follows the other as the night follows the day. God said to the early church in the Book of Revelation: "But this thou hast, that thou hatest the deeds of the Nicolaitans, which I also hate" (Rev. 2:6). You see, my friend, God loves, but also God hates. It is like the flavor of sweet and sour developed by Chinese and European chefs to a fine art. God is love but, by the same token, God is hate. And Scripture adequately states the case.

The number seven in the Bible indicates not perfection but completeness. God has a complete hatred of these things, and they are all the works of the flesh. They are things that reveal the total depravity and the utter degradation of the human species. God has gone on record that He hates them. God denies the thesis of liberal theology that He is some sentimental and senile old man who weeps but never works, that He simply shuts His eyes to the sins of mankind and is tolerant of evil, that He forgives because He hasn't the intestinal fortitude to punish sin. God says, "I *love*," but He also says, "I *hate*."

The idea that we are to be charitable to the guilty is abroad in our land because we don't have the courage to go through with a strong program of punishment. That is the thing that is corrupting and wrecking our society today. God is willing to punish the guilty. God is not afraid of public opinion. God doesn't run from any appearance of offending men. God is no coward. God says that by no means will He clear the guilty. His laws are inviolate and inexorable.

Now let's look at this ugly and hateful brood. These belong on the hate side of God's ledger:

1. "A proud look." The literal is *eyes of loftiness*. It is the attitude that overvalues self and undervalues others. This is pride. It is that thought of the heart, that little look and that turn of the face, that flash of the eye which says you are better than someone else. God says, "I *hate* it." It is number one on His list—He puts it ahead of murder and ahead of drunkenness. God hates the proud look.

It is strange that in churches today one can get by with a proud look and no one would say a thing about it. Do you know that the first overt act of sin in heaven, the original sin, was pride? It was when Satan, Lucifer, son of the morning, said in his heart, ". . . I will ascend into heaven, I will exalt my throne above the stars of God: I will sit also upon the mount of the congregation, in the sides of the north: I will ascend above the heights of the clouds; I will be like the most High" (Isa. 14:13–14). And he is the one who came to man in the Garden of Eden and said,". . . ye shall be as gods . . ." (Gen. 3:5).

It is quite interesting that behind all psychological disturbances and psychosomatic disease there is the trunk of tree from which the abnormality springs. Do you know what that is? It is a lack of being a complete personality. It is wanting to be somebody important, wanting certain status symbols—one of which is independence of God. It is wanting to be one's own god. It is making the little self to be God. That is the reason a salvation by works appeals to men. Little man likes to say, "I'm going to earn my own salvation. I'll do it myself, and I don't need You, God. I certainly don't need to have Your Son die for me. When I come into Your presence, I want You to move over because I am just as good as You are, and I'm going to sit down right beside You." My friend, a work-salvation is the result of folk who are psychologically sick. God resists the proud, and He has respect unto the lowly. He says that He will bring down the high looks. God said to Job, "Look on every one that is proud, and bring him low; and tread down the wicked in their place" (Job 40:12).

In the beatitudes of the Sermon on the Mount, the Lord Jesus said, "Blessed are the poor in spirit: for theirs is the kingdom of heaven" (Matt. 5:3, italics mine). This is what the psalmist says: "LORD, my heart is not haughty, nor mine eyes lofty: neither do I exercise myself in great matters, or in things too high for me" (Ps. 131:1). We need to take the lowly place and say, "Oh God, I am weak. I can't make it. I need You."

The other day I saw a young man walk into a group of young men. He was a big, swaggering, baby boy—that is what he was. He wanted to be accepted by his peers; so he walked in, looked around, and began to curse like a sailor. I thought, *Poor little fellow! What a poor little baby he is, trying to make himself acceptable with the other fellows. Why doesn't he simply go before God and tell Him the truth?* Psychologically man adopts all this phony stuff. How much better off he would be to say to God as the psalmist said, "Lord, my heart is not haughty. I don't want to make claims that are not genuine. I don't have any righteousness." When you go to God for His salvation, that is when you become a real, full-fledged personality. Listen to what God said through Isaiah: ". . . but to this man will I look, even to him that is poor and of a contrite spirit, and trembleth at my word" (Isa. 66:2). If you are willing to come to God on that basis, God will receive you. He hates a proud look.

2. God hates a "lying tongue." Have you ever noticed that there is far more said throughout the Bible about the abuse of the tongue than is said about the abuse of alcohol? The abuse of the tongue is something that is common to all races and all languages. People talk about a tongues movement. There is a big tongues movement today. Do you know what that is? It is the lying tongue. How tragic it is!

The psalmist (probably David) said, "I said in my haste, All men are liars" (Ps. 116:11). Dr. W. I. Carroll used to tell us in class, "David said in his haste that all men are liars. I've had a long time to think it over, and I still agree with David." I'll admit that I agree with David, too. Again the psalmist said, "Deliver my soul, O LORD, from lying lips, and from a deceitful tongue" (Ps. 120:2). In David's prayer of confession, he said, "Behold, thou desirest *truth* in the inward parts: and in the hidden part thou shalt make me to know wisdom" (Ps. 51:6, italics mine). God is the God of truth. "Into thine hand I commit my spirit: thou hast redeemed me, O LORD God of *truth*" (Ps. 31:5, italics mine). How wonderful that is. How different from the lying tongue!

3. The third thing God hates is "hands that shed innocent blood." A murderer is particularly odious and objectionable both to God and to man. God says the murderer should be punished because he took that which God said is sacred—the human life. The popular idea today is completely opposite. After a man has been killed the murderer is brought to trial, then suddenly *the murderer's life* is considered to

be precious. God says that human life is precious and that when a murderer kills a man, he is to forfeit his own life. That is the teaching of the Word of God.

4. The fourth thing God hates is "an heart that deviseth wicked imaginations"—thoughts of iniquity. I think all mankind has evil thoughts. The Lord Jesus said, "For out of the heart proceed evil thoughts, murders, adulteries, fornications, thefts, false witness, blasphemies" (Matt. 15:19). It is an ugly brood that comes out of the human heart. By the way, have you ever confessed to God what you have in your mind and in your heart? We all need to do that. We need to be cleansed.

God is dealing with the anatomy of evil and iniquity. It includes the eyes, the tongues, the hands, the heart, and the feet, as we shall see next.

5. "Feet that be swift in running to mischief." The heart blazes the trail that the feet will follow. Isaiah put it like this: "Their feet run to evil, and they make haste to shed innocent blood: their thoughts are thoughts of iniquity; wasting and destruction are in their paths" (Isa. 59:7). These are the things on God's hate list.

6. "A false witness that speaketh lies." It is not an uncommon thing today for people to perjure themselves. It seems to be one of the common sins of our time. It is a thing which God hates.

7. "He that soweth discord among brethren." There is a beatitude, given by our Lord, that looks at it from the positive side: "Blessed are the peacemakers: for they shall be called the children of God" (Matt. 5:9). There are multitudes of folk sowing discord, and they are not all politically motivated. They are in your neighborhood, and chances are they are in your church. You may even have one in your home, and there is a possibility that he even may be sitting where you sit. My friend, causing trouble between family members or brothers in Christ or fellow workers is something that God *hates*.

This list of seven sins is like a mirror. We look into it, and we squirm because we see ourselves. May I ask you to take a good look at yourself in this mirror of the Word of God. After you and I see ourselves as we really are, let us go to God and make a confession of these things. Let us be honest with Him and ask Him for His cleansing.

> My son, keep thy father's commandment, and forsake not the law of thy mother:
>
> Bind them continually upon thine heart, and tie them about thy neck.
>
> When thou goest, it shall lead thee; when thou sleepest, it shall keep thee; and when thou awakest, it shall talk with thee [Prov. 6:20-22].

The young man has grown and has gone away to school, but he is reminded not to forget the things that were taught him by his father and his mother. The things He has learned in the home are very important. He is to keep them constantly before him.

> For the commandment is a lamp; and the law is light; and reproofs of instruction are the way of life [Prov. 6:23].

WARNING AGAINST SEX SINS

Now he comes back to the great sin in our contemporary society—the sex sins.

The warning again concerns the strange woman, the prostitute. It is that which can wreck the life of a young man more than anything else. The sex sins, the sins of adultery are the great sins of our day. No one can calculate the lives that have been absolutely wrecked and ruined because of them. Oh, how many marriages are broken up today because of them! Hollywood, novels, popular songs all play on the same old theme, the triangle. There is the married couple and the third party, man or woman, who is breaking up the marriage. Proverbs has much to say about them.

> To keep thee from the evil woman, from the flattery of the tongue of a strange woman.
>
> Lust not after her beauty in thine heart; neither let her take thee with her eyelids [Prov. 6:24-25].

Notice that the young man is not to lust after her beauty in his heart. We have just learned, "Keep thy heart with all diligence; for out of it are the issues of life" (Prov. 4:23). Also notice how the young man is warned against her flattery, her beauty, her fluttering eyelids. Jesus said, "Ye have heard that it was said by them of old time, Thou shalt not commit adultery: But I say unto you, That whosoever looketh on a woman to lust after her hath committed adultery with her already in his heart" (Matt. 5:27–28). The whole sinful thought begins down in the human heart.

> **For by means of a whorish woman a man is brought to a piece of bread: and the adulteress will hunt for the precious life [Prov. 6:26].**

How many men have been ruined like that? I think we would all be shocked if we knew how many office "wives" there are. We have no idea of the number of people who are blackmailed today because of illicit sex. We hear of only a few. Just recently it was disclosed that a doctor in San Francisco had another wife and family in Southern California. Everyone who knew him thought that he was leading a moral, upright life. All the while he was keeping up two homes. This same kind of thing has happened in the lives of ministers! How does it all get started? The Lord says it begins in the heart—He made us and He knows us. "Lust not after her beauty in thine heart." It begins there.

Now he asks a few pointed questions:

> **Can a man take fire in his bosom, and his clothes not be burned? [Prov. 6:27].**

The answer to that is obvious.

> **Can one go upon hot coals, and his feet not be burned? [Prov. 6:28].**

We know of fanatics who try this, but it always burns their little tootsies to walk on hot coals.

So he that goeth in to his neighbour's wife; whosoever toucheth her shall not be innocent [Prov. 6:29].

If a man commit adultery, he is not innocent. He has no plea whatsoever. Now notice the illustration—

Men do not despise a thief, if he steal to satisfy his soul when he is hungry [Prov. 6:30].

If a man steals because he is hungry, our sympathy goes out to him. A man was arrested for stealing in my community recently, and it was found that he had some little children at home who were hungry. In a case like that you don't judge him, you want to help him. "Men do not despise a thief, if he steal to satisfy his soul when he is hungry."

But if he be found, he shall restore sevenfold; he shall give all the substance of his house [Prov. 6:31].

He can mortgage his house to repay it.

But whoso committeth adultery with a woman lacketh understanding: he that doeth it destroyeth his own soul [Prov. 6:32].

Again I draw an illustration from my own locality. A man walked into another man's room the other day, drew a gun, and shot the man dead. Why? Well, when the story came out, the man was exonerated. His home had been absolutely destroyed by the lust of the man he killed. "Whoso committeth adultery with a woman lacketh understanding: he that doeth it destroyeth his own soul."

A wound and dishonour shall he get; and his reproach shall not be wiped away [Prov. 6:33].

Committing adultery is something that will scar his soul for life. As a pastor (and I'm sure many other pastors know cases like this) I know a wife whose husband had an affair years ago; he repented of it, came back to her, and asked to be forgiven. She forgave him. But I happen to know the home, and I can see that it is not a happy home. Adultery is something you don't rub out. If you commit it, you lack understanding. You'll wreck your home; you will wreck your life.

> **For jealousy is the rage of a man: therefore he will not spare in the day of vengeance.**
>
> **He will not regard any ransom; neither will he rest content, though thou givest many gifts [Prov. 6:34–35].**

Oh, my friend, what tragedies result from adultery!

CHAPTER 7

This chapter continues the subject of chapter 6. The whole thought is to beware of a woman with easy morals.

> **My son, keep my words, and lay up my commandments with thee.**
>
> **Keep my commandments, and live; and my law as the apple of thine eye.**
>
> **Bind them upon thy fingers, write them upon the table of thine heart.**
>
> **Say unto wisdom, Thou art my sister; and call understanding thy kinswoman [Prov. 7:1–4].**

Now having said that, he is going to get right down to cases.

> **That they may keep thee from the strange woman, from the stranger which flattereth with her words [Prov. 7:5].**

He takes an illustration out of life.

> **For at the window of my house I looked through my casement,**
>
> **And beheld among the simple ones, I discerned among the youths, a young man void of understanding,**
>
> **Passing through the street near her corner; and he went the way to her house,**
>
> **In the twilight, in the evening, in the black and dark night [Prov. 7:6–9].**

This young man is taking a walk on the wrong street.

> And, behold, there met him a woman with the attire of
> an harlot, and subtil of heart.
>
> (She is loud and stubborn; her feet abide not in her
> house:
>
> Now is she without, now in the streets, and lieth in wait
> at every corner.)
>
> So she caught him, and kissed him, and with an impu-
> dent face said unto him,
>
> I have peace offerings with me; this day have I payed my
> vows [Prov. 7:10–14].

Notice that she is religious! She leads him to believe that she is right
with God—"I have peace offerings with me . . . I payed my vows."

> Therefore came I forth to meet thee, diligently to seek
> thy face, and I have found thee [Prov. 7:15].

In other words, I've been looking for you all my life, and at last I have
found you!

> I have decked my bed with coverings of tapestry, with
> carved works, with fine linen of Egypt.
>
> I have perfumed my bed with myrrh, aloes, and cinna-
> mon.
>
> Come, let us take our fill of love until the morning: let us
> solace ourselves with loves.
>
> For the goodman is not at home, he is gone a long jour-
> ney:
>
> He hath taken a bag of money with him, and will come
> home at the day appointed [Prov. 7:16–20].

She assures him that the man of the house is out of town and won't be back until a certain day.

> **With her much fair speech she caused him to yield, with the flattering of her lips she forced him.**
>
> **He goeth after her straightway, as an ox goeth to the slaughter, or as a fool to the correction of the stocks;**
>
> **Till a dart strike through his liver; as a bird hasteth to the snare, and knoweth not that it is for his life [Prov. 7:21–23].**

What a picture this is!
Now he gives the warning—

> **Hearken unto me now therefore, O ye children, and attend to the words of my mouth.**
>
> **Let not thine heart decline to her ways, go not astray in her paths.**
>
> **For she hath cast down many wounded: yea, many strong men have been slain by her.**
>
> **Her house is the way to hell, going down to the chambers of death [Prov. 7:24–27].**

This warning is to be taken literally, and there is also a spiritual application for you and me today. The Scriptures have a great deal to say about spiritual adultery. God called it that when His people left Him and went after idols. They were snared by idolatry, and they were brought into subjection. They departed from the living and true God. They were to be joined to Him, but they had separated from Him. They were actually playing the harlot; they were being unfaithful and untrue to Him. That is spiritual adultery.

Today we have many cults and "isms" and all types of false religions around us. Here in Southern California we are larded with this type of thing on every hand. For example, one says, "You don't need any longer to follow Christ as you are following Him. You don't need to trust Him alone as your Savior. What you need to do is join our group and do certain things."

You would be amazed at the letters that come to me. Some time ago I was teaching Galatians, and at that time I made the statement again and again, "Faith plus nothing equals salvation." I emphasized that you must be absolutely, utterly cast upon Jesus Christ as your Savior. Oh my, did I get the letters! A great many people wrote some very ugly things. Among other things they wrote, "You said that the Mosaic Law is something that we should get rid of." I did not say anything of the kind. What I said was that the Law cannot save you. The Law was never given to save. The Law is good, but there is something wrong with us, and only Christ can save us. When we turn from our own efforts, from our own works and turn to Him, we can be saved.

Then there were others who wrote to tell me how wrong I was. "You should have said it is necessary to be baptized in a certain way." Others said, "You should have told them to join a certain group." Others said I should have taught that we must all keep the Mosaic Law—even if a person trusts in Christ he still must keep the Law.

May I answer this by saying that the believer is joined to Christ. Christ has said we are to keep His commandments if we love Him, and His commandments are not grievous. We are to love one another. We are to be filled with the spirit of God. We are to witness to the world. Those are His commandments today. We are joined to a living Christ; we live on a higher plane. The fruit of the Spirit should be evident in our hearts and lives.

Today there is that flattering "ism" and that flattering cult, made up like a woman of the street. She is flattering and she is calling men and women. This old gal is busy today. She knocks at your door and hands out tracts. She meets you everywhere. She is a prostitute—she wants to take you away from Christ. She wants to bring you into her system. Oh, my friend, that spiritual prostitute is out on your street today; she even comes into your home by way of radio and television, trying to lure you. We are told that to follow her is like an ox going to slaughter. It is like a fool going to the correction of the stocks. Oh, that we might not settle for anything less than the person of Jesus Christ!

In my judgment this is the finest picture we have of cults, "isms," and all false religions. Like the prostitute, they are all dressed up— attractive, alluring, offering something to man that will actually destroy him and send him down to hell, and take him away from Jesus Christ, the lover of our souls.

CHAPTER 8

The young man has been examining the literature of the different colleges; and the school of wisdom and the school of fools are bidding for his application. In this chapter it is wisdom that sends out an invitation to him with a note of urgency. Pressure is put upon the young man now. The school bell is going to ring before long, and they want this young man enrolled.

WISDOM CALLS TO THE YOUNG MAN

Doth not wisdom cry? and understanding put forth her voice? [Prov. 8:1]

As we have seen, the young man has been lured and enticed to leave the school of wisdom. Believe me, the cults and "isms" are out on the streets and ringing doorbells.

God's people should be out doing the same thing. I am very thankful for the very fine organizations that especially work with the young people today. They are out ringing doorbells. They are out doing personal witnessing. That's good. Wisdom and understanding should be putting forth their voice.

She standeth in the top of high places, by the way in the places of the paths.

She crieth at the gates, at the entry of the city, at the coming in at the doors.

Unto you, O men, I call; and my voice is to the sons of man [Prov. 8:2–4].

This is what we are trying to do by radio. We are sending out a call to come to the school of wisdom. We want you to come to wisdom in the person of Christ. It is Christ who has been made unto us wisdom.

O ye simple, understand wisdom: and, ye fools, be ye of an understanding heart [Prov. 8:5].

Are you willing to take that position—to admit that you are not adequate, to say you are a sinner and that you really don't have intellectual problems? Sometimes I think it is a joke to listen to folk with "intellectual" problems. A young fellow came to me and said, "I have intellectual problems about the Bible." Do you know what he really had? He had a sin problem, and he didn't want to give up his sin. I have discovered that if a person has a sin problem and will turn to Christ with that problem, it is amazing how often the intellectual problems will be solved.

Hear; for I will speak of excellent things; and the opening of my lips shall be right things [Prov. 8:6].

What a picture we have here!

For my mouth shall speak truth; and wickedness is an abomination to my lips.

All the words of my mouth are in righteousness; there is nothing froward or perverse in them [Prov. 8:7–8].

Many people talk about errors and problems in the Bible. There are several books written about problem Scriptures. I recognize that to an intelligent person there are problems in the Bible. I had a lot of problems with the Bible at the beginning of my study, and I still have a few. But the problem is not in the Word of God. The problem is in the mind and heart of man. God says there is nothing twisted or perverse in the words of wisdom.

They are all plain to him that understandeth, and right to them that find knowledge [Prov. 8:9].

You see, if it is really wisdom, it is going to be simple, and it will appeal to the simple. I'm thankful that God did not make the gospel appeal only to folk who have a high I. Q. If He had, many folk would be left out completely. This is a message to the simple. And it really is a simple message.

It is very interesting that some things which men call deep and profound are not really that at all. When I went through school, I had the viewpoint of a lot of other young fellows that I knew it all. We had a brilliant man come to lecture at our seminary. I'll be very frank with you, he was speaking right over the top of my head. I went to the man who was considered the most brilliant professor in the school and said, "I'm not getting very much out of those lectures. I must confess that they are over my head. I always had the viewpoint that I could understand anything that any man had to say, but I am not getting what he is saying." I shall never forget his answer. He said, "Mr. McGee, you know that when water is clear, you can see right to the bottom of the pool even if it is sixty feet deep, but when the water is muddy, you can't even see to the bottom of a hoofprint in the middle of the road. Some men are not deep; they are muddy." Well, that answered it for me. My friend, if you have an intellectual problem with something you read in the Bible—let me be very frank with you—the problem is not with the Bible; the problem is with you.

Let me refer you to a passage in the New Testament, which I think is profound, although it is very simple: "And not as Moses, which put a veil over his face, that the children of Israel could not stedfastly look to the end of that which is abolished: But their minds were blinded: for until this day remaineth the same veil untaken away in the reading of the old testament; which veil is done away in Christ" (2 Cor. 3:13–14). You may be thinking, *If they cannot understand because there is a veil over their minds, they are not responsible.* And a great many folk today are claiming that there is a veil over their minds and they are not able to understand the Bible. But notice the next verses: "But even unto this day, when Moses is read, the veil is upon their heart. Nevertheless when it shall turn to the Lord, the veil shall be taken away" (2 Cor. 3:15–16). What does it mean by "it" when it says "when *it* shall turn to the Lord"? Well, it refers back to the last principal subject, which is the "heart." It is saying that when the *heart* shall turn to the Lord, the veil shall be taken away. You see, the problem is not head trouble; it is *heart* trouble.

Let's get right down to where the rubber meets the road, right down to where we live. Don't say that there are intellectual problems which keep you from the Lord. The problem is sin in your life—there are things in your life that you do not want to change. You are not willing to bow your heart and your head and come to Jesus Christ. That is the problem. Notice that when the *heart* shall turn to the Lord an amazing thing happens—the veil shall be taken away. The problems are resolved.

A great man of the Middle Ages said, "I had many problems until I came to Christ." We may call them intellectual problems, but they are really heart problems. The Word of God is clear. The gospel message is so simple it cannot be misunderstood. But there can be deliberate, willful resistance to the gospel. That is a problem of the heart.

That is why we can actually use the Word of God as a sort of Geiger counter. A Geiger counter will tell a man where there is uranium. And the reaction to the Word of God will tell a man where there is a believing heart. There are some individuals who love the Word of God, and the arrow of the counter jumps up and down. There are others who have a pious expression and fundamental vocabulary but who register as dead. They actually resist the Word of God.

Many times people have asked me to deal with folk who resist the Word of God. I tell them that my job is simply to give out the Word. The Lord Himself will deal with them. During my years in the ministry I have seen how the Lord deals with such people. I have seen Him move into families and deal with this one and that one. I recall a very arrogant young man who was questioning the Word of God. Then he left his wife and ran off with another woman. There was sin in his life; that was his problem. I emphasize this because God's Word is clear. There is nothing twisted or perverse in the words of God.

> Receive my instruction, and not silver; and knowledge rather than choice gold.
>
> For wisdom is better than rubies; and all the things that may be desired are not to be compared to it [Prov. 8:10–11].

When you and I come to the place, as Job did, where we get our priorities straight, when we put a proper evaluation on the things of this world and realize that wisdom is better than rubies, then we will put God first in our lives. It is as the Lord Jesus said, "But seek ye first the kingdom of God, and his righteousness; and all these things shall be added unto you" (Matt. 6:33).

THE CHARACTERISTICS OF WISDOM

> I wisdom dwell with prudence, and find out knowledge of witty inventions [Prov. 8:12].

The Word of God is going to make it clear that wisdom is a person, the person of the Lord Jesus Christ.

> The fear of the LORD is to hate evil: pride, and arrogancy, and the evil way, and the froward mouth, do I hate [Prov. 8:13].

We might translate it as "the mouth of perversions do I hate." This is something that is quite real today; it is right down where we live. Wisdom is manifest. It is the character of God, and that character has been revealed in Christ. Evil, pride, arrogance, and an evil way are hateful to Him. If we belong to Him, we will hate these things also.

> Counsel is mine, and sound wisdom: I am understanding; I have strength.
>
> By me kings reign, and princes decree justice.
>
> By me princes rule, and nobles, even all the judges of the earth [Prov. 8:14–16].

In the Psalms and in the prophecy of Daniel it is repeated that "the most High ruleth in the kingdom of men, and giveth it to whomsoever he will." How tremendous it is to realize that God overrules down here in the affairs of this world. Regardless of how godless a nation is, God is overruling, and His will is being accomplished. He rules in the kingdoms of men.

I love them that love me; and those that seek me early shall find me [Prov. 8:17].

Solomon learned this early in his life. He discovered that when he sought God, God gave him wisdom. He had sought God early—as soon as he became king. He knew it was God who had given him a unique wisdom. And God is prepared to give us wisdom if we are willing to meet the conditions: a diligent study and love of the Word of God early in our Christian life.

Riches and honour are with me; yea, durable riches and righteousness.

My fruit is better than gold, yea, than fine gold; and my revenue than choice silver [Prov. 8:18–19].

These are not stocks or bonds or real estate, but wonderful spiritual gifts He bestows.

I lead in the way of righteousness, in the midst of the paths of judgment:

That I may cause those that love me to inherit substance; and I will fill their treasures [Prov. 8:20–21].

WISDOM PERSONIFIED IN CHRIST

From this point on, I think you will discover that the Lord Jesus Christ is speaking.

The LORD possessed me in the beginning of his way, before his works of old [Prov. 8:22].

This is the Lord Jesus; this is wisdom personified.

I was set up from everlasting, from the beginning, or ever the earth was [Prov. 8:23].

"I was set up" is I was *anointed* from everlasting. This is the One who is the subject of John's prologue: "In the beginning was the Word, and the Word was with God, and the Word was God. The same was in the beginning with God" (John 1:1–2). He was begotten, not in the sense of having a beginning of life, but as being one nature and substance with the Father. Way back yonder in eternity He was God, and He was in the beginning with God. He was in the beginning that *has* no beginning, because "in the beginning *was* the Word." He was already past tense at the time of the beginning.

He is the One and the only One who can make this clear to us. The Lord Jesus said, ". . . no man knoweth the Son, but the Father . . ." (Matt. 11:27). We could not know the Lord Jesus, had not the Father and Son sent the Holy Spirit to open our hearts. A saved person can rest in and adore the person of Christ. We are living in the midst of great unbelief in our day, but let the skeptic be skeptical. My friend, our relationship is a personal relationship with the Lord Jesus Christ, and He is the Word. ". . . the Word was with God, and the Word was God" (John 1:1). What a tremendous statement!

Wisdom is Jesus Christ.

When there were no depths, I was brought forth; when there were no fountains abounding with water.

Before the mountains were settled, before the hills was I brought forth:

While as yet he had not made the earth, nor the fields, nor the highest part of the dust of the world.

When he prepared the heavens, I was there: when he set a compass upon the face of the depth [Prov. 8:24–27].

"All things were made by him; and without him was not any thing made that was made" (John 1:3).

"When he set a compass upon the face of the depth." It is interesting that the scientists used to speak of a square universe, but God has always said it is a circle. You and I live in a world that is round, and we are going around our planetary system. And we belong to a galactic system which is a circle. All of these circles are circling around!

When he established the clouds above: when he strengthened the fountains of the deep:

When he gave to the sea his decree, that the waters should not pass his commandment: when he appointed the foundations of the earth [Prov. 8:28–29].

Have you ever stood by the seashore and wondered why the water doesn't run over? Why does it stay where it is? It says, "he gave to the sea his decree, that the waters should not pass his commandment." God has made a law that keeps the sea right where it is.

Then I was by him, as one brought up with him: and I was daily his delight, rejoicing always before him;

Rejoicing in the habitable part of his earth; and my delights were with the sons of men [Prov. 8:30–31].

Without the Lord Jesus was not anything made that was made. All things were made by Him. He is the firstborn of all creation. He is superior to all. Why? Because by Him the Father brought all things into being, for He is the uncreated God, and He was "rejoicing always before Him." These wonderful delights and joys come to us through the amazing grace of God. How wonderful all of this is!

Now therefore hearken unto me, O ye children: for blessed are they that keep my ways.

Hear instruction, and be wise, and refuse it not [Prov. 8:32–33].

Wisdom is Christ, and there must be a love for Him.

> **Blessed is the man that heareth me, watching daily at my gates, waiting at the posts of my doors.**

> **For whoso findeth me findeth life, and shall obtain favour of the LORD [Prov. 8:34–35].**

"Whoso findeth me findeth life." If you have Christ you have life.

> **But he that sinneth against me wrongeth his own soul: all they that hate me love death [Prov. 8:36].**

My friend, if you hate Christ, you love death. What a picture this is! Wisdom is Christ.

CHAPTER 9

W e have come now to the place where wisdom has opened school. The young man is matriculated into the school of wisdom, and we are thankful for that. Everything is prepared, and we are able to look into this school. The school bell is about to ring.

THE COLLEGE OF WISDOM

Wisdom hath builded her house, she hath hewn out her seven pillars:

She hath killed her beasts; she hath mingled her wine; she hath also furnished her table.

She hath sent forth her maidens: she crieth upon the highest places of the city,

Whoso is simple, let him turn in hither: as for him that wanteth understanding, she saith to him,

Come, eat of my bread, and drink of the wine which I have mingled [Prov. 9:1–5].

W isdom has builded a house. This is the College of Wisdom. Note there are seven pillars. Those seven pillars represent to me completeness. The school offers a complete education all the way through to the graduate course and the Ph.D. degree.

Let's not minimize the importance of a good education. There are some who like to point out the Lord Jesus chose for His disciples twelve men who were not educated men. I have had many letters, one in particular from a man who took me to task for using the title of Doctor. He pointed out that none of the twelve had a doctoral degree. May I say that an *earned* doctoral degree represents years of hard work, and I believe that the person who has earned the degree is entitled to use the title. I will freely admit that one does wonder at some things in our educational system. I know a young man who is working on his master's degree in history. He is told to forget about dates and individuals, in order to get the *flavor* of a particular age—the life-style and the attitude of that period! Now I admit that that is a pretty slippery type of education. I believe that facts are important. And I know we still have some very fine schools which are working on that principle.

As far as the education of the apostles is concerned, anyone who spent three years with the Lord Jesus Christ was not uneducated. They learned a great deal from the greatest Teacher the world has ever seen. And, of course, the apostle Paul was well educated in the schools of his day. No one could say that he was an ignorant man. Let's remember that wisdom is the Lord Jesus Christ, and He can give you a complete education.

"She hath killed her beasts; she hath mingled her wine; she hath also furnished her table." Now it is time to come to school and start feasting on the courses that have been prepared.

"She hath sent forth her maidens: she crieth upon the highest places of the city." What a picture is given here. May I remind you that we have the same invitation in this age. A wedding feast has been prepared, and the invitations go out to all the invited guests saying that all things are ready. Many of the guests decline the invitation. Then the servants go out into the highways and byways with the invitation to the wedding feast (Matt. 22:1–14). It is interesting that wisdom must go out into the highways and byways to invite people to come in. And we are to go out on the highways and byways. Our message today is: God is reconciled to you; now you be reconciled to God. "Now then we are ambassadors for Christ, as though God did beseech you by us: we pray you in Christ's stead, be ye reconciled to God" (2 Cor. 5:20). In our day the Word is probably going out more than it ever has in the history of the world. The invitation is going out to the ends of the earth to come to the school of wisdom, that is, to come to the Lord Jesus Christ.

Forsake the foolish, and live; and go in the way of understanding [Prov. 9:6].

There are those who will not hear. They are the scorners. There is no use wasting your time with them. In practically every church you will find a little group that will resist the Word of God. Are we to keep on giving the Word of God to them? No. The Lord Jesus said not to cast our pearls before swine. Now notice the next three verses. Some Bible expositors think they do not belong here, that they have been inserted. But, my friend, this is exactly where they *do* belong.

He that reproveth a scorner getteth to himself shame: and he that rebuketh a wicked man getteth himself a blot.

Reprove not a scorner, lest he hate thee: rebuke a wise man, and he will love thee.

Give instruction to a wise man, and he will be yet wiser: teach a just man, and he will increase in learning [Prov. 9:7-9].

If you give the Word of God to some people, they will actually hate you for it. This is a pattern that has been true down through the ages. There are people who are so shallow, empty, and ignorant that they will not receive the Word of God at all.

In our day we hear about the man who is liberal in his theology and how broad-minded he is. Did you know that it is the "broad-minded" liberal who has put religion out of our schools? They call the fundamental people bigots. I'd like to know who is the real bigot! Frankly, I don't mind evolution being taught in our schools if they will permit me to teach the Bible alongside it. But the broad-minded liberals will not allow that. Regardless of the degrees they hold, they are ignorant. They have narrow minds when they are not willing for the Word of God to be taught. The general rule is that the less a man knows, the more he thinks he knows. I have never met a liberal yet who didn't think he was a very smart cookie. He thought that he knew and understood it all; yet he doesn't understand. The more a man really knows, the more he will recognize his ignorance and his limitations. One of the truly great preachers whom I have known—and I think he had one of the best minds of any man I have ever met—often said, "The more I study the Bible the more I recognize how ignorant I am of it." My friend, you cannot study the Bible without realizing how ignorant you are of it.

However, the scorner has no interest in learning the Word of God. You waste your time by giving it to him.

The fear of the LORD is the beginning of wisdom: and the knowledge of the holy is understanding [Prov. 9:10].

Perhaps you are saying, *We've had this verse before.* Yes, when the little fellow was in the home, the first lesson he was given was the fear of the Lord. "The fear of the LORD is the beginning of knowledge: but fools despise wisdom and instruction" (Prov. 1:7). Now he has entered the college of life and the college of wisdom; he is in his freshman year of the university of understanding, and this is his first lesson: "The fear of the LORD is the beginning of wisdom: and the knowledge of the holy is understanding." That is where we all start. If you haven't started there, you haven't started, my friend. A man is a fool (which is what this book will say) to live without God in this world.

In our contemporary society we are so concerned with safety—safety on the highway, safety in the home, security in old age. We carry insurance for all these things, and we make sure our premiums are paid up. That is the wise thing to do. But, my brother, what about eternity? Are you making any plans; do you have insurance for that? Oh, how foolish it is to live this life without God! "The fear of the LORD is the beginning of wisdom."

For by me thy days shall be multiplied, and the years of thy life shall be increased.

**If thou be wise, thou shalt be wise for thyself: but if thou
scornest, thou alone shalt bear it [Prov. 9:11–12].**

If you want to be smart, then make preparation for your soul for eternity. If you are going to be a scorner and ridicule all of these things,
well, you are coming up for judgment. This may sound crude, but
somebody ought to say it: you are on your way to hell. "If thou
scornest, thou alone shalt bear it." If you are determined to go on in
your own way, you will be the loser.

The town atheist in a place where I preached said to me, "You
know, preacher, I don't buy this stuff about eternal life and trusting
Jesus and all that sort of thing. It may be all right for some folk, but I
don't care for that." I answered, "Let's suppose you are right and there
is no eternal life, then you and I will come out at exactly the same
place. But suppose I am right and you are wrong. Then, my friend,
you are in a pretty bad spot." Another atheist said, "I would be content
if it weren't for the awful fact that the Bible may be true." Yes, it may
be! And if it is, it will be an awful fact for anyone who turns his back
on God.

THE SCHOOL OF THE FOOLISH WOMAN

**A foolish woman is clamorous: she is simple, and
knoweth nothing [Prov. 9:13].**

You see, foolishness runs a school also. There are a lot of those
around today.

**For she sitteth at the door of her house, on a seat in the
high places of the city [Prov. 9:14].**

She doesn't have to go out on the highways and byways to invite folk
in; they come to her. Thousands are going to schools like this!

Whoso is simple, let him turn in hither: and as for him that wanteth understanding, she saith to him,

Stolen waters are sweet, and bread eaten in secret is pleasant.

But he knoweth not that the dead are there; and that her guests are in the depths of hell [Prov. 9:16–18].

Oh, how many so-called wise men have turned in there and found a tragic end! It was Lord Byron who wrote toward the end of a life of debauchery:

> My days are in the yellow leaf;
> The flowers and fruits of love are gone;
> The worm, the canker, and the grief
> Are mine alone!

Byron had everything this world can offer—good looks, genius, fame, wealth, and yet he said, "the worm, the canker, and the grief are mine alone!" That is what the school of the foolish woman did for him.

A famous movie star here in California had been married to several of the beauties of the world during his life. The other day, as an old man, he committed suicide, leaving this note: "I am bored with life." How tragic.

May I say to you, foolishness still runs a college, and there is a long waiting list of those who clamor to enter. "But he knoweth not that the dead are there; and that her guests are in the depths of hell."

CHAPTER 10

PROVERBS OF SOLOMON, WRITTEN AND SET IN ORDER BY HIMSELF

This begins the second major division of the Book of Proverbs. Here we see that the young student is given some guidelines for his life. These are lessons that you and I also are to learn in the school of Christ.

> **The proverbs of Solomon. A wise son maketh a glad father: but a foolish son is the heaviness of his mother [Prov. 10:1].**

"A wise son maketh a glad father." Have you ever noticed that when a father has a son who has gone to school and made good grades or been outstanding as an athlete or in some other accomplishment, the old man goes around and brags about his son and tells everyone about him? "My boy has his Ph.D. and is teaching in college." "My boy is on the football team." But suppose the boy failed or didn't make the team. Then the father becomes very quiet and doesn't say anything about him at all. He just keeps his mouth shut.

"But a foolish son is the heaviness of his mother." It is the mother who grieves at a time like that. The father just keeps quiet about it and ignores it. What a picture of life this is! A boy can be a wise son or a foolish son—either one.

> **Treasures of wickedness profit nothing: but righteousness delivereth from death [Prov. 10:2].**

"Treasures of wickedness profit nothing"—men who have accumulated a great fortune have had to leave it here. They couldn't take it with them, and they never really enjoyed it while they were alive.

"Righteousness delivereth from death." Christ has been made unto us not only wisdom but righteousness. And ". . . whosoever believeth in him should not perish, but have everlasting life" (John 3:16).

> **The LORD will not suffer the soul of the righteous to famish: but he casteth away the substance of the wicked [Prov. 10:3].**

You will remember that I have mentioned that I think there is a proverb for everyone, and a proverb that fits certain characters in the Bible. When we remember that "The LORD will not suffer the soul of the righteous to famish," we think of Joseph. He was sold into Egypt and must have felt that he had come to the end and that God seemed far away. Yet he had faith in God. We know that God did not forsake him. God so arranged it that eventually he was brought out of prison and was made the prime minister of the land of Egypt.

> **He becometh poor that dealeth with a slack hand: but the hand of the diligent maketh rich [Prov. 10:4].**

What a difference there is in people. Some wonderful Christians are so generous, and others are so stingy! It is interesting that the tight individual has that kind of life—he seems uptight all the time. By contrast, the generous man has a full life.

Don't you think this verse would fit Abraham? He was a generous man. He told his nephew Lot, "Take any part of the land you want, and I'll take what is left." It is a very generous man who will divide real estate like that! Abraham had the right to do the choosing. He certainly knew that the choice land was the well-watered plain of Jordan. Lot must have thought Abraham was very foolish not to move down there, but since Abraham had given Lot the opportunity to choose, he chose the rich land down there in the plain. With a very slack hand, very selfishly, he chose the best for himself; but, in the end, he lost everything.

"But the hand of the diligent maketh rich." There are two words that won't go together in the Bible: faith and laziness will not mingle. A lazy Christian is not a Christian with real faith in God. The one who is diligent is the one who will work, the one who will *labor*. This reminds me also of the apostle Paul. When the Lord called him, He certainly did not get a lazy individual.

> **He that gathereth in summer is a wise son: but he that sleepeth in harvest is a son that causeth shame [Prov. 10:5].**

Here is another proverb of contrast. The boy who is called "wise" is the one who works in the summer. The lazy boy is the one who sleeps during the time of harvest. He is not the one who is going to get the job done.

My young Christian friend, you need to recognize that God wants to train you and school you. When I was young, I was the pastor in a little church. I wasn't satisfied; I wanted to do more for God than I was doing there. I have a wonderful wife who encouraged me to finish working on my doctor's degree and devote time to studying the Bible. I was redeeming the time; I took advantage of that period. How I thank God for it! After I became very busy pastoring a large church and carrying a radio and conference ministry, someone asked me, "You are so busy all the time, when are you able to do your preparation?" Well, back in a little town in Texas I had five years, and I spent that time studying. And the day came when God enabled me to use that preparation. I would say to any young person today who wants to be used of God: begin to prepare yourself. Remember that "he that gathereth in summer is a wise son."

These statements in the Book of Proverbs are tremendous, eternal truths. They are truths not to send you soaring into the heavenly places, but to equip you for the sidewalks of your own town. If they are not working for *you*, there is nothing wrong with them, but there is something wrong with you.

> **Blessings are upon the head of the just: but violence covereth the mouth of the wicked [Prov. 10:6].**

What a picture we have here of two men in the Old Testament. "Blessings are upon the head of the just" reminds me of Samuel. "But violence covereth the mouth of the wicked (lawless)" reminds me of Saul.

The memory of the just is blessed: but the name of the wicked shall rot [Prov. 10:7].

I think of this in connection with certain individuals who a few years ago were famous, but today they are fading out. I am of the opinion that men of this generation will be forgotten in the next fifty years. Yet the memory of men such as Dwight L. Moody, who accomplished something for God, lives on.

The wise in heart will receive commandments: but a prating fool shall fall [Prov. 10:8].

"Prating" is literally *word-mouthing*—he is the one who is always talking. He is wise in his own conceit. By contrast, the wise in heart will *receive* commandments. Remember there was a king by the name of Nebuchadnezzar who listened to the counsel of Daniel and prospered. There was another king by the name of Belshazzar. He was a fool. A royal banquet one night marked the end of him and his kingdom (Dan. 5).

He that walketh uprightly walketh surely: but he that perverteth his ways shall be known [Prov. 10:9].

This is expressed in our proverb today: Honesty is the best policy.

He that winketh with the eye causeth sorrow: but a prating fool shall fall [Prov. 10:10].

Here is something that is quite interesting. The eye and the mouth shall be in agreement. When you see a man say something and wink, it means he doesn't mean what he said. His mouth and his mind are not in agreement. When they are not in agreement, it will cause a great deal of sorrow.

Whom does this verse fit? How about Judas? The kiss of Judas certainly was a kiss of betrayal. The kiss is meant to denote affection, but it certainly didn't mean that for him.

In the lips of him that hath understanding wisdom is found: but a rod is for the back of him that is void of understanding [Prov. 10:13].

The whole world came to hear the wisdom of Solomon, but "a rod is for the back of him that is void of understanding" characterizes his son Rehoboam. He would not listen to the advice of the wise old men; he listened to the young men who had grown up with him (1 Kings 12). As a result, he brought division and civil war to his nation.

Wise men lay up knowledge: but the mouth of the foolish is near destruction [Prov. 10:14].

All the time the wise man is gathering up knowledge, the foolish man has one foot in the grave and the other on a banana peel.

The labour of the righteous tendeth to life: the fruit of the wicked to sin [Prov. 10:16].

This proverb makes me think of Cain and Abel. "The labour of the righteous tendeth to life." Abel raised sheep, and he brought a little lamb for his sacrifice. "The fruit of the wicked (the produce of the lawless) to sin." That was Cain—in rebellion he brought the fruit of the ground. The apostle Paul expressed it this way in Romans 8:6: "For to be carnally minded is death . . ."—and this is directed to the Christian. "Death" for him means separation from God in the way of fellowship. God is not going to fellowship with a carnally-minded person. When the proverb says "the labour of the righteous tendeth to life," it is fellowship with God. Abel was a saved man. "The fruit of the wicked (lawless) to sin" characterized Cain.

**He is in the way of life that keepeth instruction: but he
that refuseth reproof erreth [Prov. 10:17].**

This would apply to Absalom, David's son. He wouldn't accept reproof. He made a big mistake in attempting to seize the kingdom from
his father.

**He that hideth hatred with lying lips, and he that ut-
tereth a slander, is a fool [Prov. 10:18].**

What a terrible thing it is to have someone pretend to be your friend
and later you discover that he is really your enemy. That person is
actually a fool. You catch on to him after a while. Anyone who slan-
ders is also a fool.

God had given a specific commandment regarding this. "Thou
shalt not go up and down as a talebearer among thy people . . ." (Lev.
19:16). It goes on. "Thou shalt not hate thy brother in thine heart: thou
shalt in any wise rebuke thy neighbour, and not suffer sin upon him"
(Lev. 19:17). Don't flatter a man when you actually hate him, but neither are you to slander the man.

This describes a man in Scripture. Remember that Joab pretended
to be a friend to Abner. He lured him out of the city, and then he killed
him.

**The lips of the righteous feed many: but fools die for
want of wisdom [Prov. 10:21].**

I think again of Samuel, the great judge of Israel, in contrast to Saul,
the king who played the fool.

**The blessing of the LORD, it maketh rich, and he addeth
no sorrow with it [Prov. 10:22].**

There are those who live in pleasure and think they are living it up.
But as they get closer to the end, they find life unbearable. I watched a
banquet, a political affair, that was televised. All who attended the

banquet were rich, and they were there for the purpose of supporting the party with a contribution. The thing I noticed was that there wasn't a happy face in the crowd. The camera panned the entire audience. I thought, *My, here they are at a banquet and jokes are being told, but I don't see a single happy face.*

"The blessing of the LORD, it maketh rich, and he addeth no sorrow with it." The contemporary Christian by his indifference to moral and doctrinal wrong, and by his laxness in his way of living, is missing a great deal that God has for him.

> **It is as sport to a fool to do mischief: but a man of understanding hath wisdom [Prov. 10:23].**

This is good advice to the young man!

> **As vinegar to the teeth, and as smoke to the eyes, so is the sluggard to them that send him [Prov. 10:26].**

Did you ever send a lazy boy on an errand, and then you stand first on one foot and then on the other waiting for him? That's just like "vinegar to the teeth, and as smoke to the eyes."

> **The fear of the LORD prolongeth days: but the years of the wicked shall be shortened [Prov. 10:27].**

This certainly was true in Old Testament days. God promised long days to those who obeyed Him. Perhaps you are thinking, *Doesn't He promise that today?* No, He promises us eternal life. That will be a better quality of life as well as quantity.

> **The righteous shall never be removed: but the wicked shall not inhabit the earth [Prov. 10:30].**

Let's look at history with that in view. All of the great world leaders, the kings and the captains, have disappeared. The pharaohs, the Caesars, Alexander the Great, Napoleon—they are all gone. "The wicked shall not inhabit the earth." Neither will communism prevail and, interestingly enough, neither will democracy, because God has a form of government that is to be a monarchy. There will be no dictatorship equal to the dictatorship of Jesus Christ when He takes over the rulership of this earth. And "the righteous shall never be removed."

CHAPTER 11

As we have seen, the young man is in college now, and wisdom—which is Christ—is the Teacher. Wisdom had to go out on the highways and byways to get her pupils, but she has a class now, and she is teaching by proverbs.

The literary form of these proverbs is mostly couplets. The two clauses of the couplet are generally related to each other by what has been termed parallelism, according to Hebrew poetry. Hebrew poetry is attained by repeating or contrasting a thought. There are three types of parallelism: synonymous parallelism that restates the thought of the first clause; antithetic parallelism which gives contrasting truths; and synthetic parallelism in which the second clause develops the thought of the first.

This chapter will actually give the young man some good advice about business.

A false balance is abomination to the LORD: but a just weight is his delight [Prov. 11:1].

God does enter into business; you can take Him into partnership with you. However, you can't form a partnership with Him if you are crooked. If you are honest, He would like to be your partner.

The Christian businessman is to be honest and a man of integrity. I am thankful that there are so many of these wonderful Christian businessmen. I have played golf with such a man. He lives in Chicago but had come down to Florida to attend our Bible conferences. Although we became well-acquainted, I didn't come to know much about him in his business dealings. I was so pleased when another man who knows him well told me that this man is known far and near for his honesty and integrity. And he is a successful businessman. It is wonderful to find there are still men like this.

**When pride cometh, then cometh shame: but with the
lowly is wisdom [Prov. 11:2].**

The other besetting sin is pride. Immediately here in his freshman
course the young man is warned about pride. This proverb contrasts
pride and humility. Always with pride comes "shame." There is a
great deal in Scripture, and especially in this Book of Proverbs, about
pride.

**The integrity of the upright shall guide them: but the
perverseness of transgressors shall destroy them [Prov.
11:3].**

This simply means that if a person wants to walk in the truth, if that is
the desire of his heart, the spirit of God can be counted upon for guidance and direction. The contrast is: the "perverseness of transgressors
[the treacherous] shall destroy them."

The other evening I talked with a young man who has the same
problem that I had when I was going to school, which was finances.
He asked me, "How do you tell the will of God; how do you know the
way you should go?" My answer was this: "I had the same problem
that you have. Always for me it narrowed down to only one way, and it
would become very simple. The way that opened up was the way that
I could go. If the door were closed, it was closed. If I didn't have the
money to go to school, I simply would not go. But it seemed the Lord
would always open up just one door to let me go in. That happened to
me again and again, and I always interpreted it as an open door from
the Lord. I believe that if you mean business with God, He will open
up the door. That has been my experience."

**Riches profit not in the day of wrath: but righteousness
delivereth from death [Prov. 11:4].**

Doesn't this remind you of the Lord's account of the rich man and the
beggar named Lazarus? Both of them died. The riches of the rich man

didn't avail him anything in the day of wrath. But righteousness delivered the beggar; it took him right to Abraham's bosom.

Those who trust riches certainly have their priorities upside down. There is nothing wrong in wealth, but we need to recognize that it has limitations. Money will buy almost anything in this world, but it can buy nothing in the next world.

> **The righteousness of the perfect shall direct his way: but the wicked shall fall by his own wickedness.**

> **The righteousness of the upright shall deliver them: but transgressors shall be taken in their own naughtiness [Prov. 11:5–6].**

Perhaps it will mean more to us if we translate "wicked" by the word *lawless*.

> **When a wicked man dieth, his expectation shall perish: and the hope of unjust men perisheth.**

> **The righteous is delivered out of trouble, and the wicked cometh in his stead [Prov. 11:7–8].**

"When a lawless man dieth, his expectation shall perish: and the hope of unjust men perisheth." Doesn't this remind you of Haman in the Book of Esther? And Mordecai was the righteous man "delivered out of trouble."

> **An hypocrite with his mouth destroyeth his neighbour: but through knowledge shall the just be delivered [Prov. 11:9].**

Hypocrite comes from the two Greek words meaning "to answer back." The hypocrite is one who answers back, and the word was used for actors in Greek plays. When one actor would give the cue to the other actor, he knew it was time for him to say his little piece. It was play-acting. To say a man is a hypocrite in religious matters means that he is a phony. He is the man who will say "Hallelujah, praise the Lord" insincerely. He is just playing a part; he is not praising the Lord in his heart.

"An hypocrite with his mouth destroyeth his neighbour." He will pretend to be your friend, but he will knife you when your back is turned in an attempt to cover up the sin in his own life. Whom do you think of in the Bible in this connection? Wouldn't it be Potiphar's wife and the way she maligned Joseph? She brought false charges against Joseph to cover up her own sin. She was the guilty party, but she covered it over by accusing Joseph. Who would believe the story of a slave against the story of the wife of an official of Pharaoh? There was no need for Joseph to even open his mouth, because he didn't have a chance to defend himself.

Unfortunately, sometimes in the church we find a hypocrite who will say terrible things in order to protect himself. I have always been afraid of the man who is nice to his preacher to his face but who criticizes him behind his back. I have always felt that I needed to watch out for that kind of man. He is covering up something in his own life. Time has demonstrated to me that this was often a correct estimation of the situation. This proverb is referring to this kind of hypocrisy.

When it goeth well with the righteous, the city rejoiceth: and when the wicked perish, there is shouting.

By the blessing of the upright the city is exalted: but it is overthrown by the mouth of the wicked [Prov. 11:10–11].

I place David and Saul beside these proverbs. When David was king of Israel, Jerusalem became a great city. When King Saul died, there was not much mourning for him.

He that is void of wisdom despiseth his neighbour: but a man of understanding holdeth his peace [Prov. 11:12].

I believe David is an example of this proverb, too. Did you ever stop to think of the tremendous effect the life of David had upon Solomon? Even though David had committed sin with Solomon's mother, Bathsheba, David's life was a wonderful life except for that blot on it. You remember when David had to flee from the city when Absalom rebelled against him, that Shimei, of the family of Saul, cursed him. Old Joab, David's captain, wanted to go over and run a spear through him. David said, "No, he is speaking out of his heart. This is God's judgment upon me." "A man of understanding holdeth his peace."

There will be times when you will find folk are actually cursing you, maligning your character. Just keep quiet. The Lord will take care of it, as He took care of this situation with David.

These are wonderful principles in this book. They are good for young people to study. There seems to be a real spiritual movement among the young people of today. I would like to see them study the Book of Proverbs. It would bring them to Christ, because He is the One who runs the school of wisdom and He is made unto us wisdom. Proverbs would give young people a lot of common sense. It seems to me we are short on common sense today. We seem to have a lot of high I. Q.'s and a lot of low common sense quotients.

> **A talebearer revealeth secrets: but he that is of a faithful spirit concealeth the matter [Prov. 11:13].**

A talebearer is one who tells something in order to hurt someone else. Sometimes the thing he is saying is true, but he still ought not to say it to others. If he knows that a brother has sinned, he ought to go to him personally and deal with him privately about it. He should not run around and tell everyone else about it.

> **Where no counsel is, the people fall: but in the multitude of counsellors there is safety [Prov. 11:14].**

Perhaps a more understandable translation is this: "Where no management is, the people fall: but in the multitude of counsellors there is safety." Regardless of how smart you are, you need good advice. You will remember that God gave Daniel to be an adviser to Nebuchadnezzar. He helped his king a great deal. Daniel was also an adviser to Cyrus, and he was a great help to him.

> **He that is surety for a stranger shall smart for it: and he that hateth suretyship is sure [Prov. 11:15].**

One who goes surety for a stranger shall smart for it, and he will get smart from the experience. He will learn that he made a big mistake.

However, there was One who was surety for a stranger. Do you know who that was? Well, listen to the apostle Paul, "For ye know the grace of our Lord Jesus Christ, that, though he was rich, yet for your sakes he became poor, that ye through his poverty might be rich" (2 Cor. 8:9). He assumed your debt of sin, and mine. He had to pay the awful penalty. His experience is described prophetically in Psalm 69:4: "They that hate me without a cause are more than the hairs of mine head: they that would destroy me, being mine enemies wrongfully, are mighty: then I restored that which I took not away." And again, "He was oppressed, and he was afflicted, yet he opened not his mouth: he is brought as a lamb to the slaughter, and as a sheep before her shearers is dumb, so he openeth not his mouth" (Isa. 53:7). The penalty was exacted, and He became answerable for it. The ". . . wages of sin is death . . ." (Rom. 6:23) and Christ paid it for me. What a wonderful thing that is! Dr. H. A. Ironside in *Notes on the Book of Proverbs*, p. 121, wrote:

> He bore on the tree the sentence for me;
> Now both the Surety and sinner are free.

He took my place.

> **A gracious woman retaineth honour: and strong men retain riches [Prov. 11:16].**

This reminds me of Ruth in the Book of Ruth. She was a widow, she was poor, and she was a woman. Yet she retained her honor. Boaz could say to her, ". . for all the city of my people doth know that thou art a virtuous woman" (Ruth 3:11). The whole town of Bethlehem knew her. Not only did she maintain her honor in relationship with the opposite sex, but in every way she retained honor. The second part would apply to Boaz. "And strong men retain riches."

> The wicked worketh a deceitful work: but to him that soweth righteousness shall be a sure reward.
>
> As righteousness tendeth to life: so he that pursueth evil pursueth it to his own death.
>
> They that are of a froward heart are abomination to the Lord: but such as are upright in their way are his delight.
>
> Though hand join in hand, the wicked shall not be unpunished: but the seed of the righteous shall be delivered [Prov. 11:18–21].

Here is quite a contrast between sin and righteousness. Deceitfulness and lawlessness are going to be judged—there is no escape. And the righteousness which a believer has is the righteousness of Christ. Because we have that, we will not come into judgment but will pass ". . . from death unto life" (John 5:24).

Now here is a choice proverb—

> As a jewel of gold in a swine's snout, so is a fair woman which is without discretion [Prov. 11:22].

Have you ever seen a pig walking around with a gold ring in its snout? Well, there are a lot of them out here in Hollywood, California. They are beautiful women with no discretion.

> The desire of the righteous is only good: but the expectation of the wicked is wrath [Prov. 11:23].

The only way to have peace and joy is to be rightly related to Christ.

> There is that scattereth, and yet increaseth; and there is
> that withholdeth more than is meet, but it tendeth to
> poverty.
>
> The liberal soul shall be made fat: and he that watereth
> shall be watered also himself [Prov. 11:24–25].

This is a paradox. Dr. Ironside put it like this:

> Bunyan's quaint rhyme, propounded as a riddle by Old Honest,
> and explained by Gaius, is in itself a suited commentary on
> these verses:
>
> > A man there was, though some did count him mad,
> > The more he cast away, the more he had.
> > He that bestows his goods upon the poor
> > Shall have as much again, and ten times more.

The Lord has said that if one sows sparingly, he shall also reap sparingly. That is a general principle. It certainly also applies to giving to the work of the Lord.

> He that withholdeth corn, the people shall curse him:
> but blessing shall be upon the head of him that selleth it
> [Prov. 11:26].

This verse reminds me of Joseph down in Egypt. He didn't withhold the corn. He gathered it faithfully for seven years and then he was able to feed the world, including his own father and brothers and their families.

It also reminds me of Nabal—"he that withholdeth corn" certainly applies to him. He was a fool, and that is what his name means. He was married to a beautiful woman, Abigail. Why she married him, I don't know, except that he was a rich man. David, during the years he was hiding from Saul, had taken care of Nabal's sheep and had helped him on many occasions. So when David and his men were hungry, he called on Nabal for food. Nabal turned him down flat—in fact, he insulted the messengers whom David had sent. (Redheaded David would not take that lying down! He went after the man, but on his way Abigail came to meet him with an offering of peace.) This proverb fits Nabal like a glove.

Also I believe we could give this proverb a spiritual application. The corn is the Word of God. Many preachers are withholding the corn. They preach on political issues and social questions instead of teaching the Word of God. God have mercy on preachers who are withholding the corn from their people!

We *all* are to give out the corn today—this is not just for the preachers. Are you sitting on the sidelines, withholding corn from those around you? You could be a great impetus in getting a teaching of the Word of God into your area. Oh, my friend, "He that withholdeth corn, the people shall curse him." But what a thrill it is to have someone come and thank you for bringing them the Word of life! "Blessing shall be upon the head of him that selleth it"—or *giveth* it without money and without price.

> **He that diligently seeketh good procureth favour: but he that seeketh mischief, it shall come unto him [Prov. 11:27].**

This is another evidence that ". . . whatsoever a man soweth, that shall he also reap" (Gal. 6:7).

> **He that trusteth in his riches shall fall: but the righteous shall flourish as a branch [Prov. 11:28].**

When our Lord gave parables, which I believe he drew from real life, He told about a farmer who had such a bumper crop that he decided to tear down his barns to build bigger barns. He would give all his attention to that. There is nothing wrong in building bigger barns, but the Lord said that he was a fool, because he was so interested in building big barns down here that he didn't think of building anything for eternity. That is the danger of riches. No one can buy his way into heaven.

The fruit of the righteous is a tree of life; and he that winneth souls is wise [Prov. 11:30].

Many years ago a survey was conducted on the sons of preachers, because P.K.'s (preacher's kids) come in for a lot of criticism. It was found that several United States presidents were sons of preachers, including Woodrow Wilson. Also some of our outstanding scientists were sons of preachers. Generally the children of saved folk turn out very well.

Today there seems to be a flurry of little courses on how to achieve harmony in the home. I wish we could get past that smattering of knowledge and the little surface coating that is being applied today. A little course in psychology about being sweet and nice in the home is not the answer. We need to return to the Word of God and to living a godly life in the home. A lot of our family problems would evaporate if we had righteousness in the home. "The fruit of the righteous is a tree of life."

"He that winneth souls is wise." Today a great deal of attention is being given to personal witnessing. That is good. I believe it is one of the finest things that is taking place in our day and generation. The Word of God has been saying all the time, "he that winneth souls is wise."

Behold, the righteous shall be recompensed in the earth: much more the wicked and the sinner [Prov. 11:31].

Judgment is coming. There can be no doubt about that.

CHAPTER 12

In the school of wisdom, the boy is still in his freshman year, but the instruction is very important.

> **Whoso loveth instruction loveth knowledge: but he that hateth reproof is brutish [Prov. 12:1].**

The man who loves instruction is a man who has a true estimate of what is top priority and what is really of superior value. That means that he will listen to instruction. However, I must say that after getting folk to listen to the Word of God, one of the great problems is getting them to obey what it says. Obedience is absolutely essential.

> **A good man obtaineth favour of the LORD: but a man of wicked devices will he condemn [Prov. 12:2].**

Psalm 1:5 tells us that ". . . the ungodly shall not stand in the judgment, nor sinners in the congregation of the righteous." Regardless of fame or riches or standing high in the estimation of men, the ungodly man will come to a sorry, sad ending. God is certainly going to judge such men. "A man of wicked devices will he condemn."

> **A man shall not be established by wickedness: but the root of the righteous shall not be moved [Prov. 12:3].**

Our Lord gave a parable that deals with this. In the Sermon on the Mount, He told about a man who built his house on a rock, and another who built his house on the sand (Matt. 7:24–27). The rock, of course, symbolizes Christ, the solid foundation of the Word of God.

Now here in his freshman course, the young man is given advice about choosing a wife.

A virtuous woman is a crown to her husband: but she that maketh ashamed is as rottenness in his bones [Prov. 12:4].

Think of the wonderful wives who are mentioned in the Old Testament. Eve must have been a wonderful person in spite of the fact that she listened to the serpent. Sarah was a model wife according to 1 Peter 3:6. The mother of Moses, Jochabed, was undoubtedly a remarkable woman.

Then there are others who were not so good and could be described as "rottenness in his bones." Job's wife was not much of a help to him. It is interesting that Satan took away from Job everything that he leaned upon except his wife, which must mean that Satan knew she wasn't very much help to Job. Then there was bloody Athalia whose mother was the wicked Jezebel. So there are many illustrations in the Scriptures of this proverb.

Ogden Nash gave advice on how to make marriage a success in a little poem that he wrote:

> To keep your marriage brimming
> With love in the loving cup,
> Whenever you're wrong, admit it;
> Whenever you're right, shut up.

That is good advice, by the way.

The thoughts of the righteous are right: but the counsels of the wicked are deceit.

The words of the wicked are to lie in wait for blood: but the mouth of the upright shall deliver them.

The wicked are overthrown, and are not: but the house of the righteous shall stand [Prov. 12:5–7].

Again let me change the word *wicked* to *lawless,* which is probably more accurate. You can see that God believes in law and order. He has a great deal to say about lawlessness.

> A man shall be commended according to his wisdom:
> but he that is of a perverse heart shall be despised [Prov.
> 12:8].

"Shall be despised" is literally "shall be exposed to contempt." I think of Gideon and his son. Gideon is to be commended according to his wisdom. Abimelech, his son, was exposed to contempt.

> He that is despised, and hath a servant, is better than he
> that honoureth himself, and lacketh bread [Prov. 12:9].

This proverb is rather confusing, but it seems that a contrast is being made. Another translation reads: "Better is the poor that provideth for himself." The thought appears to be that the one who is looked down upon as being lowly, but whose needs are met, is far happier and more to be envied than he who delights in appearing prosperous while feeling the pinch of poverty.

> A righteous man regardeth the life of his beast: but the
> tender mercies of the wicked are cruel [Prov. 12:10].

As I have mentioned, my father was killed in an accident in a cotton gin when I was fourteen years old. I was at the age when a boy thinks his dad is a hero, and, frankly, I have never gotten over it. I remember one time we were driving on a dirt road by horse and buggy from Ardmore to Springer, Oklahoma. Ahead of us was a man in his buggy who was drunk and was beating his horse. We couldn't get around him, and my dad got out of our buggy and talked to the man about beating his animal. Of course the man, being drunk, was offended and took a swing at my dad, but he missed him. So my dad hit him and knocked him down. He took the whip away from him and told him to get back in his buggy and let his horse alone. Then we followed him as he went on ahead of us. This incident impressed me, and I am delighted to find in Scripture a proverb like this: "A righteous man regardeth the life of his beast."

A man who owns several dogs told me that he always judges a man by the reaction of his dogs to that man. Dogs seem to know character. They know whether they would be mistreated by an individual. It is interesting that the animal world seems to be able to judge human character better than some of us do.

> **He that tilleth his land shall be satisfied with bread: but he that followeth vain persons is void of understanding [Prov. 12:11].**

This proverb is saying to stay on the job, keep busy, and don't do so much running around.

All the way through this chapter we have contrasts like this:

> **The wicked desireth the net of evil men: but the root of the righteous yieldeth fruit [Prov. 12:12].**

There is repetition in this section for emphasis. After all, repetition is the best kind of teaching, if you can get by with it. If you keep saying a thing, your pupil will never forget it.

> **The way of a fool is right in his own eyes: but he that hearkeneth unto counsel is wise [Prov. 12:15].**

You know to whom this refers, I am sure. It is Rehoboam, the son of Solomon. He refused the wise counsel of the older men in his kingdom, which resulted in his own downfall and civil war in his nation.

> **He that speaketh truth sheweth forth righteousness: but a false witness deceit.**
>
> **There is that speaketh like the piercings of a sword: but the tongue of the wise is health [Prov. 12:17–18].**

My friend, if your pastor is preaching the truth, there are times when he is going to put the sword right in your heart. And if you are not willing to accept it—well, the hypocrite always covers up with hatred and bitterness. This is the reason I am always a little afraid of a man who is highly critical of his pastor—that is, if he is nice to his face but is sticking a knife in his back.

> **The lip of truth shall be established for ever: but a lying tongue is but for a moment.**
>
> **Deceit is in the heart of them that imagine evil: but to the counsellors of peace is joy.**
>
> **There shall no evil happen to the just: but the wicked shall be filled with mischief [Prov. 12:19–21].**

All of these verses have to do with the tongue, the lying tongue and the lips of truth. They are put in contrast. The Word of God has more to say about the tongue, more judgment on the abuse of the tongue, than it has to say about the use and abuse of alcohol. Yet it is interesting that a lying tongue and a gossip can get by in Christian circles today, whereas a drunkard would be rejected.

> **Lying lips are abomination to the LORD: but they that deal truly are his delight [Prov. 12:22].**

One of the things that should characterize a child of God is his truthfulness.

> **A prudent man concealeth knowledge: but the heart of fools proclaimeth foolishness [Prov. 12:23].**

A prudent man will not say things that are going to hurt someone. But you have probably been in a crowd where there is some foolish person, a big-mouthed person, who says something that casts a reflection on another person—of course, someone who is not present in the crowd. The prudent man would not say it, but the heart of the fool will say things like that.

The hand of the diligent shall bear rule: but the slothful shall be under tribute [Prov. 12:24].

I believe that in our contemporary society this has been somewhat turned around. It is not always the diligent who are elected to office, and I'm not sure it is the slothful who are paying the taxes. At least I don't want to come in under the category of being lazy, and I certainly pay taxes. I have asked God for light as I have studied these proverbs, and I have come to realize that some of them should be considered in the light of eternity. I believe that the measuring stick for this proverb is eternity rather than a local situation. Aren't we told that someday we are going to rule with Christ? But Scripture does not teach that all believers will rule equally; there will be gradations. I personally would be very embarrassed if I found myself on the same plane as the apostles, sitting next to the apostle Paul. I don't belong there. However, I do think that the *diligent* are to rule with Christ.

Heaviness in the heart of man maketh it stoop: but a good word maketh it glad [Prov. 12:25].

Job said to his friends, "How forcible are right words! . . ." (Job 6:25). Right words can bring comfort and cheer and encouragement to those who are grieving or who have a problem or have bitterness of spirit. We certainly are not to beat down a person who is having problems. We are to give him a good word.

The righteous is more excellent than his neighbour: but the way of the wicked seduceth them [Prov. 12:26].

It would be clearer to translate it this way: "The righteous searcheth out his neighbor." The righteous man wants to help his neighbor, while the lawless man will try to hurt his neighbor. The righteous man will come to talk to a neighbor and face him if he finds he is wrong. That is the most helpful thing he can do.

Nathan was the best friend David had; yet it was Nathan who had

the courage to point his finger at David and say, ". . . Thou art the man
. . ." (2 Sam. 12:7). When there are things in our lives that need to be
straightened, it is wonderful to have a good friend who will reprove us
in love.

One of the best friends I ever had was a man who helped me
through school. When I first started in the ministry, the Lord was gracious to me and let me be pastor of a church that had been my home
church, where the people loved me and were very sympathetic with
me. I was pretty much of an amateur to be pastor of such a large and
prominent church in that day. They were good to me.

I went to a conference at Winona Lake and heard a man speak who
I thought was great. I came back and tried to imitate him. I even tried
to imitate his accent! My church membership discovered that. They
just sat there and smiled, very few said anything about it, and I received no harsh criticism. However, this man who had helped me
through school invited me to lunch. He said just one thing that I shall
never forget, and it was a good proverb. "Vernon, we would rather
have a *genuine* Vernon McGee than an *imitation* anybody else." That
was all he said. Friend, that is all he needed to say. From then on, I
went back to being Vernon McGee—that may not have been *good*, but
it was better than trying to imitate somebody else. How forcible are
right words! The righteous will search out his neighbor and help
him—that is exactly what this man did for me. But the wicked (the
lawless) seduceth them. He goes over and pats him on the back and
then crucifies him when his back is turned. These proverbs gear right
down into your neighborhood, right down into your church, right
down into your place of work, don't they?

> **The slothful man roasteth not that which he took in
> hunting: but the substance of a diligent man is precious
> [Prov. 12:27].**

I find this proverb quite humorous. This fellow went out and shot a
deer, but he was too lazy to skin the deer and cut up the meat and cook
and eat it. You must be pretty lazy to be that kind of hunter. It's like the
fisherman who will fish but won't clean the fish to eat them.

"But the substance of a diligent man is precious." In other words, he takes care of what he has.

Remember when Ruth went out to glean in the field and Boaz was so generous with her that she had a surprising amount; then she beat out the grain that she had gleaned. She could have come home and thrown the gleanings down in front of Naomi and said, "Look what I have done. I worked hard all day for this. Now you can beat it out." She didn't do that. This reveals the kind of spirit that was in her.

Men, it won't hurt you to help with some of the work at home. You can even do the dishes now and then. I have learned that, since I am retired and at home more, I have become a member of the "Honey-do Club." It is, "Honey, do this," and "Honey, do that." When I was a boy I used to tell my mother, "When I grow up I'm never going to wash dishes again." Well, I must be in my second childhood, because I'm washing dishes again.

In the way of righteousness is life; and in the pathway thereof there is no death [Prov. 12:28].

A wonderful vista opens to the child of God! Physical death is ahead of us if the Lord tarries, but eternal life is out yonder.

CHAPTER 13

W e continue in this section where we are learning some of the great principles of life.

> **A wise son heareth his father's instruction: but a scorner heareth not rebuke [Prov. 13:1].**

Although Solomon was not David's favorite son, Solomon did at least listen to him. He is an example of a wise son who heard his father's instruction. Rehoboam, the son of Solomon, is an example of the scorner who did not listen. He is an example to us of the dark side or the negative side, as we have found in many of these proverbs. But there are other examples that we could find in Scripture.

> **A man shall eat good by the fruit of his mouth: but the soul of the transgressors shall eat violence.**
>
> **He that keepeth his mouth keepeth his life: but he that openeth wide his lips shall have destruction [Prov. 13:2–3].**

There is a type of talking today which is gossip; it is foolish talking. It borders on being risqué—telling things that have a double meaning. The double entendre joke even gets into Christian circles today. And when they do, they seem to dwell on this matter of sex.

I have noticed that many of these folk take courses on sex, and then later on I hear that their home was broken up. The husband has run away with another woman and all that sort of thing. I believe much of this trouble is a result of such borderline living and borderline speaking. That is the thing we are warned about here, and the young man is told to beware of it.

> **The soul of the sluggard desireth, and hath nothing: but**
> **the soul of the diligent shall be made fat [Prov. 13:4].**

You will remember that the apostle Paul put it right on the line to the Thessalonians. There were some pious souls there who said, "We're looking for the Lord to come," and they quit work. Paul wrote, ". . . if any would not work, neither should he eat" (2 Thess. 3:10). Let's not be doling out food to those who will not work. We are to work. And if you really believe that the Lord is coming, it will make you a better worker.

> **A righteous man hateth lying: but a wicked man is**
> **loathsome, and cometh to shame.**

> **Righteousness keepeth him that is upright in the way:**
> **but wickedness overthroweth the sinner [Prov. 13:5–6].**

This refers to truth in the inward parts. This is the background of practical righteousness. God hates that which is false; He cannot tolerate it. The child of God should recognize and deal with any sin in his life. This old nature of ours is inclined to lie. It just comes naturally to us to lie. God says He hates that, and He will have to deal with that type of thing.

> **There is that maketh himself rich, yet hath nothing:**
> **there is that maketh himself poor, yet hath great riches**
> **[Prov. 13:7].**

Here is another example of the old nature that we all have. If we are poor we want to put up a front, to keep up with the Joneses. We pretend to have more than we actually have. Some people drive a Cadillac automobile simply to impress other folk, even though they really can't afford it. Some live in a neighborhood they really cannot afford.

On the other hand, there are people who are really very wealthy but are always talking about how *poor* they are. A member in one of

my former churches was a very wealthy man, but he probably gave
less than anyone else. He was always talking about how high prices
were and how much things cost him. And he would say he'd be broke
if things didn't get better.

Both sides are an abomination to God because each is hypocritical.
It is putting up a front that we don't need to put up. We don't need to
try to keep up with the Joneses; neither ought we to act as if we don't
even know the Joneses. We are to treat them as neighbors, and then we
ought to be just what we are.

> **The light of the righteous rejoiceth: but the lamp of the
> wicked shall be put out [Prov. 13:9].**

In the study of the history of the kings of Israel, I called attention to
this principle at work. One line after another became kings in the
northern kingdom. Then, suddenly, they were cut off, often in a violent manner by murder. This is what God says: "The lamp of the
wicked shall be put out." It happens again and again in this world.
The end of Hitler was not pretty. And the end of Stalin evidently was
not either.

> **Only by pride cometh contention: but with the well ad-
> vised is wisdom [Prov. 13:10].**

When you find contention in a group, in a neighborhood, in a church
or church group, the basis of it will be found to be pride. It is *always*
that. As someone has said, it takes two to make a quarrel—*always*.

> **Wealth gotten by vanity shall be diminished: but he that
> gathereth by labour shall increase [Prov. 13:11].**

This is another proverb that should be considered in the light of eternity; that is the yardstick that you must put down alongside this.
Many wealthy men apparently knew that they had very foolish offspring; so they established trust funds and put legal chains around

their estates so their offspring could not get to it. Such an arrangement is made so that their offspring can live off the income, but they cannot touch the estate itself. As a result there are many rich sons in the world today, men who never made a dime in their lives, they wouldn't know how to work for a living at all; yet they are heirs to tremendous fortunes. But they have been protected so that they cannot touch the principal of their estates. If they could, they would foolishly spend it all.

Now this proverb needs to be looked at in the light of eternity. What are true riches? What is wealth really? Is it those stocks and bonds? Well, the individual is going to lose them someday. Death took them away from the original owner. Nobody came in and stole them; he stole away! He went off and left them. And that's going to happen to those who own those stocks and bonds today.

> **Hope deferred maketh the heart sick: but when the desire cometh, it is a tree of life [Prov. 13:12].**

You can just keep hoping for something that doesn't come to pass—that will make the heart sick. This is the reason we ought to be in step with the will of God in our lives, because we hope for a great many things that will not be realized in our lives at all. How much better it is to accept the reality of the situation in which God has placed us!

> **Whoso despiseth the word shall be destroyed: but he that feareth the commandment shall be rewarded.**
>
> **The law of the wise is a fountain of life, to depart from the snares of death.**
>
> **Good understanding giveth favour: but the way of transgressors is hard [Prov. 13:13–15].**

All through Proverbs there is this contrast between righteousness and wickedness. God hates pride; He hates lawlessness; He hates hypocrisy. He has no use for this type of thing that arises out of our human nature. That is the reason that God will not accept anything that we do in the old nature. It is only what He can perform through our new nature that is acceptable to Him. One thing is sure: He is not going to take Vernon McGee's old nature to heaven. I'll be glad to get rid of it. In heaven you and I will be forever parted from that old nature which produces all the sins that are inherent in each of us.

God makes what He wants very clear in Isaiah 66:2: ". . . to this man will I look, even to him that is poor and of a contrite spirit, and trembleth at my word." That is the way we must all come to God if we wish to be accepted of Him. We cannot come in pride. And we dare not despise His Word nor His commandments.

A wicked messenger falleth into mischief: but a faithful ambassador is health [Prov. 13:17].

We have had men in our government who have had access to government secrets, to that which is "top drawer" as far as the policy of this country is concerned, and some of these men have been homosexuals. When the enemy discovers this, it makes it possible for them to use these men. The same is true about men who have a weakness for alcohol. "A wicked messenger falleth into mischief." We need men of high integrity in our government. It is important whether a man drinks or not. I think it is tragic that so many men high up in government positions use alcohol. I think that is a part of our problem as a nation today. We need to recognize that these basic proverbs which seem so simple are so important to our lives as individuals and as a nation.

He that spareth his rod hateth his son: but he that loveth him chasteneth him betimes [Prov. 13:24].

This is real child psychology. The child of God today is told the same thing. "Children, obey your parents," but the father is told, ". . . provoke not your children to wrath . . ." (Eph. 6:1, 4). That is, don't whip them or discipline them when you are angry or talking in a loud voice. Wait until a time when you can calmly sit down with your child and talk with him and explain why he is being disciplined. That is very important. This is the reason my father's discipline was so good. He often did not deal with me until maybe a day had gone by. And I thought several times I had gotten by with it, but I hadn't. He very calmly dealt with me, and I knew he was not doing what he did because he was angry. Discipline is very important.

CHAPTER 14

The Book of Proverbs is an important section of the Word of God. Here we find the wisdom of God distilled into small sentences. We see that they fit individuals who are mentioned in the Bible. Also they fit folk whom we know, and they fit you and me.

Every wise woman buildeth her house: but the foolish plucketh it down with her hands [Prov. 14:1].

"Every wise woman buildeth her house." This is not talking about the physical building of a home. I think Sarah is an example of a wife who built her house. She was the wife of a patriarch, and she built up the house of Israel. I think we can say that Jochabed, the mother of Moses, built her house. Although she was a slave in a foreign land, to save her son she hid him, watched over him, and finally became his nurse in the service of Pharaoh's daughter. She is the one who taught him about the Lord and the promise of the Lord to Israel. She was a wonderful mother, and she built her house.

"But the foolish plucketh it down with her hands." Several women in the Scriptures did that. Because of their wickedness, the house they built was destroyed. Let me point out one passage in particular. "Forty and two years old was Ahaziah when he began to reign, and he reigned one year in Jerusalem. His mother's name also was Athaliah the daughter of Omri. He also walked in the ways of the house of Ahab: for his mother was his counsellor to do wickedly" (2 Chron. 22:2–3). The counsel of his mother really brought the house of Ahab low. This is indeed a true proverb. You can take these into the laboratory of life and see them work out even today. I know of several examples of women whose personal sins have destroyed their homes.

He that walketh in his uprightness feareth the LORD: but he that is perverse in his ways despiseth him [Prov. 14:2].

This tells us that our walk will reveal our relationship with God. We are told by the apostle John, "He that saith he abideth in him ought himself also so to walk, even as he walked" (1 John 2:6). Our walk should be in obedience to the Father just as the walk of the Lord Jesus was.

You will remember that Samuel laid this matter before King Saul: ". . . Behold, to obey is better than sacrifice, and to hearken than the fat of rams" (1 Sam. 15:22). Obedience to the Lord is the important thing. Without that, your religion is phony and false.

In the mouth of the foolish is a rod of pride: but the lips of the wise shall preserve them [Prov. 14:3].

This reminds me of David and Goliath (1 Sam. 17:41–49). "In the mouth of the foolish is a rod of pride." This is a picture of Goliath. He did a lot of boasting as the champion of the Philistines. When David volunteered to fight him, Goliath reacted this way: "And the Philistine said unto David, Am I a dog, that thou comest to me with staves? And the Philistine cursed David by his gods. And the Philistine said to David, Come to me, and I will give thy flesh unto the fowls of the air, and to the beasts of the field" (1 Sam. 17:43–44).

"But the lips of the wise shall preserve them." Now notice David's answer: "Then said David to the Philistine, Thou comest to me with a sword, and with a spear, and with a shield: but I come to thee in the name of the LORD of hosts, the God of the armies of Israel, whom thou hast defied" (1 Sam. 17:45).

Where no oxen are, the crib is clean: but much increase is by the strength of the ox [Prov. 14:4].

This is a very interesting proverb. In several portions of Scripture the ox is used as an example to us. Also the ox was a beast of sacrifice, symbolic of Christ in sacrifice.

Now the ox was a strong animal. In fact, he was the tractor and the sedan of the families in that day. They used the ox to ride to market, and they used the ox to plow their fields. I suppose he was rather a dirty animal in the sense that his crib needed to be cleaned out, and that was an unpleasant task because he was a big animal. Of course, the way to get rid of cleaning the crib was to get rid of the ox. That would give them a clean crib, but they would be deprived of the "strength of the ox."

This has a tremendous spiritual lesson for us. Sometimes we try to solve problems in the church and try to clean up divisions in the church by throwing out the ox. Often there is a group or clique in the church, busy as termites and with about the same result, who want to get rid of those people who insist on having Bible teaching in the church. They are going to clean the crib, they think, so they throw out the ox. I believe this has happened to church after church in our country. After a while it becomes evident that it was the oxen who pulled the plow. They were the ones who contributed financially; they were the ones who sent out the missionaries; they were the ones who paid the bills. So before one tries to do any cleaning, it is very important to find out who are the oxen in the Lord's work.

I play golf with a wonderful Christian man. He gives to our Bible-teaching program because he believes in teaching the Bible. We have wonderful fellowship together, but we disagree on a lot of things. When we are playing golf, I like to concentrate on the game. He is always talking to me about my work, saying, "Why don't you do this, and why don't you do that?" Sometimes that is a little irritating. I could get rid of him—that would be getting the crib clean—but I would be throwing out the ox! I would lose a friend who is very right in much of the advice he gives me. And he pulls the plow with me in trying to get out the Word of God. How absolutely foolish it would be to clean the crib by throwing out the ox.

A faithful witness will not lie: but a false witness will utter lies [Prov. 14:5].

The Lord Jesus has been called the faithful and true witness. That is the kind of witness we ought to be, too.

We hear a great deal today about being a witness for Christ. There are courses given on how to be a witness for Christ. It is wonderful to take a course that will enable you to go out and ring doorbells and tell people about the Savior. But remember, there are two kinds of witnesses: the faithful and the false. If you tell someone that Jesus saves and keeps and satisfies, are you telling the truth? You answer, "Of course, it is the truth." Yes, the facts are true, but have you proven it to be true in your own life? Or are you being a false witness?

Fools make a mock at sin: but among the righteous there is favour [Prov. 14:9].

Jezebel is a prime example in the Word of God of one who made "a mock at sin." We are told to turn away from people who do that and have nothing to do with them.

The heart knoweth his own bitterness; and a stranger doth not intermeddle with his joy [Prov. 14:10].

Every heart has some secret joy or sorrow that no one can share. No one. We may try to share it, but they do not understand. I remember some folk asked me to tell them about my operation for cancer. I told them how in the hospital I had turned to God and how at that time He had made Himself real to me. They didn't like that. I could see they turned me off. Later I said to myself, *Probably that is a secret that I can't share with anyone else.*

Have you ever had some wonderful, joyful experience, and you attempted to tell it to your loved ones? When I was a young man, some time after my dad had died, I wrote a poem. At that time I was living with an aunt, and there were several relatives there. I came in and said, "Look, I've written a poem, and I want to read it to you." I read it, and it brought great joy to me, but it didn't bring any joy to them. They turned me off when I started reading it. In fact, that experience caused me to stop writing poetry. If I were a budding poet, I was lost to the world forever, because they sure put a stop to my poetry right there! There are some things we can share with others, and there are some things we cannot share.

There is a way which seemeth right unto a man, but the end thereof are the ways of death [Prov. 14:12].

This is a verse which should be applied to the cults and "isms." They sound so reasonable and so nice and so attractive. Recently a friend said to me, "Why is it that this certain cult keeps growing as it does?" I said, "Because it appeals to the old nature of man. It appeals to the flesh. It tells you that if you are a nice sweet fellow and follow certain rules, you are going to make it." My friend, "there is a way which seemeth right unto a man," but notice the end of this proverb: "but the end thereof are the ways of death." The end is eternal separation from God. How important it is to be in the right way! The Lord Jesus said, ". . . I am the way, the truth, and the life: no man cometh unto the Father, but by me" (John 14:6).

The simple believeth every word: but the prudent man looketh well to his going.

A wise man feareth, and departeth from evil: but the fool rageth, and is confident.

He that is soon angry dealeth foolishly: and a man of wicked devices is hated.

The simple inherit folly: but the prudent are crowned with knowledge [Prov. 14:15–18].

The viewpoint of the world is that the Christian is a person who has a low I. Q., is very naive, and will believe everything that is said to him. The real child of God—and the only kind of child of God is a *real* one—is not simple in that sense. He doesn't believe anything and everything.

Have you ever noticed that the disciples were constantly questioning the Lord? The man we call "doubting Thomas" was constantly raising questions. Simon Peter asked many questions: "Lord, where are You going? Why can't I follow You?" Philip, the quiet one, asked Him, "Show us the Father. That's all we need." Judas (not Iscariot) asked, "How is it You will show us these things and not show them to the world?" These fellows were always raising questions.

If you are a child of God, you will not be gullible. You're not going to swallow everything you hear. Faith is not a leap in the dark. Faith is not betting your life on something. Nor is it the little girl's definition, "Faith is believing what you know ain't so." My friend, faith rests upon a solid foundation, God says if it is not on a solid foundation, don't believe it. "The simple believeth every word." The prudent man, the wise man, tests what he hears.

The fear of the Lord causes a wise man to test what he hears. He will not be taken in. He won't believe what the preacher says just because the preacher says it. He will check what the Word of God says. I want to say to you right now that you should not believe anything I say just because I say it. I am not the oracle of Delphi; I do not speak *ex cathedra*; I am not a know-it-all. You test what I say by the Word of God. There is a lot of sweet-sounding speech going out from churches and from the media. Oh, my friend, don't believe everything you hear. Test it by the Word of God.

The poor is hated even of his own neighbour: but the rich hath many friends [Prov. 14:20].

That seems to be becoming more and more true. I doubt if a poor rail-splitter like Lincoln could run for the presidency in our day. A candidate has to be rich.

He that despiseth his neighbour sinneth: but he that hath mercy on the poor, happy is he [Prov. 14:21].

How do you feel toward those who can do nothing for you in return? Do you do something for them?

In all labour there is profit: but the talk of the lips tend-eth only to penury [Prov. 14:23].

Some people just *talk*; they don't *do*. People can almost be classified as either talking people or doing people.

The crown of the wise is their riches: but the foolishness of fools is folly [Prov. 14:24].

The riches here are not necessarily material riches. There are a great many happy people who are rich, not in the things of this life, but in those things that are spiritual. That is the most important of all.

A true witness delivereth souls: but a deceitful witness speaketh lies [Prov. 14:25].

The Lord Jesus said it this way: ". . . if the blind lead the blind, both shall fall into the ditch" (Matt. 15:14).

The fear of the LORD is a fountain of life, to depart from the snares of death [Prov. 14:27].

To teach the fear of the Lord was the object of the Holy Spirit all the way through the Book of Proverbs.

A sound heart is the life of the flesh: but envy the rotten-ness of the bones [Prov. 14:30].

How true this is! Envy will not only rob you of your joy and fellow-ship with the Lord, but it will affect you physically.

Righteousness exalteth a nation: but sin is a reproach to any people [14:34].

I wish this verse were inscribed over the United Nations instead of the verse about beating their swords into plowshares, which will not happen until Christ reigns on this earth. When Christ returns, then they will learn that righteousness *does* exalt a nation. Today the nations do not believe that righteousness exalts them, but history bears testimony to it. The pathway of history is strewn with the wrecks, the debris, and the ruins of nations that didn't follow this principle. "Sin is a reproach to any people."

CHAPTER 15

This chapter contrasts goodness and evil and emphasizes first the role of the tongue, then of the heart.

THE TONGUE

A soft answer turneth away wrath: but grievous words stir up anger [Prov. 15:1].

I'm sure that the people who come to your mind at this proverb are Abigail and Nabal. We have seen several proverbs that are applicable to them. Abigail was the beautiful, lovely wife and woman. Nabal, her husband, was the fool but a very rich man. Someone has written a book called "Beauty and the Beast," and it is the story of Nabal and Abigail—Abigail is the beauty and Nabal is the beast. You will recall that when Abigail heard that her husband had sent an insulting answer to David, who had in kindness and consideration taken care of his flocks, she hurriedly ordered the servants to gather a great deal of food for David. Then she went to meet David and fell down on her face before him. She recognized him as the future king, and she spoke to him of the fact that his life was bound up in the bundle of life with God—a beautiful expression. She gave a soft answer, and it did turn away wrath. On the other hand, grievous words stir up anger—which certainly was true of the words of Nabal.

You will notice many illustrations of this as you go through the Word of God. We find that the Lord Jesus Himself used the strongest language in the entire Scriptures in His denunciation of the Pharisees in Matthew 23. There can be a proper time to "put it on the line," and Jesus certainly could do that. But notice how gracious He was to those who needed the grace of God. He told the poor woman in sin, ". . . Neither do I condemn thee: go, and sin no more" (John 8:11). What a gracious thing to say to her. So we find illustrations of this again and again in the Word of God. There is a time for the very gracious, soft answer. There is also a time when the answer needs to be strong.

The tongue of the wise useth knowledge aright: but the mouth of fools poureth out foolishness [Prov. 15:2].

We are back again to the tongue. I'll repeat what I have said before—there is more said in the Bible about the abuse of the tongue than about the abuse of alcohol. That does not mean we commend alcohol; I think the greatest curse of this country right now is not dope or drugs but alcohol. Somehow people tend to point an accusing finger at the drug addict, but they excuse the alcoholic as being sick and needing help. He certainly does. The Word of God condemns drunkenness but even more severely condemns the abuse of the tongue. That little tongue will tell people who you really are. It will give you away. I have a little booklet entitled *Hell on Fire*. It is a scriptural title, dealing with the tongue, that dangerous little instrument.

The eyes of the LORD are in every place, beholding the evil and the good [Prov. 15:3].

You may look to the right hand and to the left hand and think that nobody is watching you. Even Big Brother may not be watching you, but God is watching. God sees you.

Remember that when Moses saw an Egyptian beating one of his brethren in slavery, he looked this way and he looked that way, and then he slew the Egyptian. He forgot to look up! He didn't think anyone knew. God knew. Your life and my life are an open book before God. What is secret sin down here is open scandal in heaven. "The eyes of the LORD are in every place, beholding the evil and the good."

A wholesome tongue is a tree of life: but perverseness therein is a breach in the spirit [Prov. 15:4].

Here is the tongue again. It can get us into a lot of trouble. It can get us out of trouble, too. It can be a blessing or a curse.

A fool despiseth his father's instruction: but he that regardeth reproof is prudent [Prov. 15:5].

There is so much said in the Book of Proverbs about listening to advice and instruction. It has been said that you can't tell a fool anything. That is true. You can tell him, but you can't get through to him for the very simple reason that he is not listening to instruction.

In the house of the righteous is much treasure: but in the revenues of the wicked is trouble [Prov. 15:6].

This contrast is not dealing with material riches. The treasure that is in the house of the righteous consists of things like joy, peace, love, sympathy, comfort—wonderful treasures. They are the great treasures of life. The contrast is with the revenues of the wicked which are trouble.

The lips of the wise disperse knowledge: but the heart of the foolish doeth not so [Prov. 15:7].

This changes the word from tongue to lips, but the meaning is still the same. The wise disperse knowledge.

The sacrifice of the wicked is an abomination to the LORD: but the prayer of the upright is his delight [Prov. 15:8].

This is a fundamental principle. The wicked cannot do good or think right. It is impossible for them to do so. Let's skip down for a moment and see another verse that states the same truth. "The thoughts of the wicked are an abomination to the LORD: but the words of the pure are pleasant words" (v. 26). The thoughts of the wicked are an abomination to the Lord and so are the sacrifices that he brings.

The reason they are an abomination is that he is wrong, wrong on the inside and wrong on the outside. He is all wrong, and whatever he does is wrong. The problem is that he has not learned to come in humility, recognizing his lost condition, coming to the Lord Jesus Christ for salvation. Someone has said, "A person who trusts so much as a single hair's breadth of his works for salvation is a lost soul." That is true. "The sacrifice of the wicked is an abomination to the LORD." A person may be religious. He may go to church and go through certain formalities, but that has no value as far as God is concerned. I do not understand why people think that if they do certain religious things, that will make them right with God. The *heart* must be changed. God does interior decorating before He can do any exterior decorating. He is not interested in *your* exterior decorating until He has done a job of interior decorating in your life.

> **The way of the wicked is an abomination unto the LORD: but he loveth him that followeth after righteousness [Prov. 15:9].**

We have seen what God thinks of the *sacrifice* of the wicked and of the *thoughts* of the wicked; now we see that the *way* of the wicked is also an abomination to the Lord. But He loves the person who follows after righteousness. Remember that it is Christ who has been made unto us righteousness (see 1 Cor. 1:30).

> **Correction is grievous unto him that forsaketh the way: and he that hateth reproof shall die [Prov. 15:10].**

A man hates to be told that he is wrong. There are some people who will not accept any kind of advice or admonition.

THE HEART

> **Hell and destruction are before the LORD: how much more then the hearts of the children of men? [Prov. 15:11].**

The Epistle to the Hebrews tells us, "Neither is there any creature that is not manifest in his sight: but all things are naked and opened unto the eyes of him with whom we have to do" (Heb. 4:13). God is the discerner of the thoughts and intents of the heart. "Hell" or Sheol, the unseen world which none of us has seen, and which the man of the world does not believe exists, is open before God.

Only God can make that unseen world real to a child of God, which will give him a true perspective of this life. The man who lives with the idea that this life is all there is has a different set of values and a different list of priorities from that which the child of God has. When we talk to people who are not the children of God, it is important to get their perspective of life, to see how they are thinking. But only God can reveal what is on the other side in the unseen world. You and I can't do that. Only the Spirit of God can take the things of Christ and make them real to us and to them.

Jesus Christ walked on this earth in the flesh over 1,900 years ago. He stepped through the doorway of death, but He was made alive on the third day. For forty days He revealed Himself to His disciples. Then He went back to glory, and He sent His Holy Spirit to us. Only the Holy Spirit of God can make Him real to us. The Lord Jesus promised that the Holy Spirit would ". . . take of mine, and shall shew it unto you" (John 16:15). It is very important for us to be aware of this.

A merry heart maketh a cheerful countenance: but by sorrow of the heart the spirit is broken [Prov. 15:13].

It is known that laughter and good cheer and joy actually add to a man's health and to the length of his life. They bring to life a wonderful dimension that cannot be there if we live in sorrow and pessimism.

The heart of him that hath understanding seeketh knowledge: but the mouth of fools feedeth on foolishness [Prov. 15:14].

Here he is emphasizing the heart rather than the head of man. He is not talking so much about the accumulating of certain facts but about spiritual discernment or, as someone has put it, "sanctified common sense." There is a dearth, a famine, of that in the land.

**Better is little with the fear of the LORD than great trea-
sure and trouble therewith.**

**Better is a dinner of herbs where love is, than a stalled
ox and hatred therewith [Prov. 15:16–17].**

A good illustration of this is found in the life of Daniel. He was taken
as a slave into Babylon when he was just a young man. He showed
remarkable ability, so he was put with the wise men to be trained for
government service. He was to be given a certain diet which he
refused to eat because it was forbidden to the Jews by the laws of God.
He asked instead for a diet of cereal. He did this because of his fear of
the Lord. He wanted to serve God. My, how God honored that man! He
made him prime minister to Nebuchadnezzar, the first great world
ruler. When the Persians took over, God again made Daniel the prime
minister to the second great world ruler, Cyrus the Great. God honored His servant.

**A wrathful man stirreth up strife: but he that is slow to
anger appeaseth strife [Prov. 15:18].**

This takes us back to verse 1. A man who is crude and rough in his
dealings will stir up strife.

However, it is also true that preaching the Word of God will stir up
strife. Remember that the Lord Jesus was the most controversial person who has ever been on this earth. Wherever the truth is preached,
strife will be the result, because there are folk who don't want to hear
it. Remember that we said the Word of God works like a Geiger
counter. If you run it over a congregation, you can learn who is a genuine Christian and who is not.

A young preacher having trouble in his congregation came to me
about it. I told him about my experience when I was a boy. When I
would go to the barn at night to feed the horse or the cow, I would light
a lantern and carry it with me. When I would open the barn door and
step in, two things would happen: The rats would scurry and run for
cover, and the birds which were roosting on the rafters would begin to

sing. Light had those two very different effects. And when the Word of God is preached you will see the rats run for cover and the birds begin to sing.

We do need to keep in mind that we are not to exaggerate the offense of the Cross—just preach it.

A wise son maketh a glad father: but a foolish man despiseth his mother [Prov. 15:20].

The father brags about his boy when he is making good. If the boy is failing, you won't hear a word out of his dad.

A man hath joy by the answer of his mouth: and a word spoken in due season, how good is it! [Prov. 15:23].

It is not only *what* you say but *when* you say it. Sometimes the right word at just the right time will do the job. Many of us could testify that the right word said to us at the right time in our lives changed the whole course of our lives. That has certainly happened to me.

The thoughts of the wicked are an abomination to the LORD: but the words of the pure are pleasant words [Prov. 15:26].

We have already seen that the sacrifices of the wicked, the ways of the wicked, and the thoughts of the wicked are an abomination to the Lord. The wicked must be turned from his wicked ways. He must be turned to God.

The LORD is far from the wicked: but he heareth the prayer of the righteous [Prov. 15:29].

Peter writes the same thing. He says that God hears the prayer—that's interesting—of the righteous; but His ears are closed to the prayer of the wicked (1 Pet. 3:12).

The light of the eyes rejoiceth the heart: and a good report maketh the bones fat [Prov. 15:30].

I tell you, one good way to lose weight is to hear a bad report, to get some bad news.

The fear of the LORD is the instruction of wisdom; and before honour is humility [Prov. 15:33].

The important lesson for man to learn is to come with humility to learn of God. We all need that lesson.

CHAPTER 16

This is a very rich and important section—short sentences drawn from long experience, tested in the crucible of time and of suffering. They are made rich and real to us by the power of the Holy Spirit. The proverbs are for all time, although they were written specifically to the young man who was an Israelite under the Mosaic Law. However, they widen out and speak to all of our hearts in a very definite way: to rich and poor, male and female, black and white. This is a book that can reach down and touch us all.

> **The preparations of the heart in man, and the answer of the tongue, is from the Lord [Prov. 16:1].**

Dr. H. A. Ironside translates this: "The purposes of the heart are of man: but from Jehovah is the answer of the tongue." Our human proverb that would go along with this is, "Man proposes, but God disposes." As the Word of God says, ". . . it is not in man that walketh to direct his steps" (Jer. 10:23). You may plan, and I may plan or arrange things, but when the time comes to speak or act, God is the One who is going to have the last word. We may make a great boast, but only God can give the final answer.

> **All the ways of a man are clean in his own eyes; but the Lord weigheth the spirits [Prov. 16:2].**

"All the ways of a man are clean in his own eyes." We have seen this before in Proverbs 14:12, "There is a way which seemeth right unto a man, but the end thereof are the ways of death."

If you have ever dealt with lost people and have spoken to them about their salvation, or if you have been a preacher or a teacher, you know the answer that you get most of the time: "I don't need to be saved. I'm all right. What is wrong with me? I'm willing to stand before God. I'm an honest man." It is that sort of thing on and on. A man is clean in his own eyes. I have had that thrown back at me even as a challenge.

There are even a great many Christians who think that their walk is perfect before God. The whole issue is wrapped up in this one verse of Scripture: "But if we walk in the light, as he is in the light, we have fellowship one with another, and the blood of Jesus Christ his Son cleanseth us from all sin" (1 John 1:7). We need to hold up the mirror of the Word of God to our lives, and it will reveal that things are not quite right, that we don't measure up to God's standard. You may measure up to the standard of the chamber of commerce, and it may make you Man of the Year; your club may reward you and give you a plaque; your church may pat you on the back; and your neighbors may say that you are a great guy. But, my friend, when you see yourself in the light of the Word of God, then you see that you have a need and that there are spots on your life. You will see that you have come short of the glory of God. Your way may be clean in your own eyes, but it is not clean in God's eyes. "If we say that we have fellowship with him, and walk in darkness, we lie, and do not the truth" (1 John 1:6). Now John is speaking to Christians. There are a great many folk sitting in a church pew as comfortable as you please. In fact, they tend to point their finger at other folk and say, "They're not so good, but I am. I'm really all right." I think some of the saints today have, in effect, asked God to move over. They want to sit next to Him and look down to judge their fellow Christians.

The way of a man may seem clean in his own eyes, but Jehovah weighs the spirit. God searches you. Have you ever seen a pair of scales that can weigh spirits? Well, I'll tell you one—the Word of God. It is a mirror. It is a set of scales to measure you, and it says that you come short, that you don't measure up.

Some folk have misunderstood what I said in our study of the Epistle to the Galatians. They write to me and say, "You said that the Mosaic Law is no good today, that the Law is inoperative." I didn't say that. What I said was that the Law cannot *save* you. The Law is *good*; Paul said it's good. It is a mirror. It reveals to you that you have come short of the glory of God. My friend, if you look at the Law of God and still say that you are measuring up to it, then you haven't really seen the Law yet. You don't really know what the Law is saying. The Law demands perfection, and you and I cannot produce it. Therefore we need a Savior. That is what the Law will do: it is a schoolmaster to bring us to Christ. It will take you by the hand and bring you to the Cross and say, "Little fellow, what you need is a Savior." The Law is good, but it will not save you. If the ways of a man are clean in his own eyes—even with the Word of God before him—may I say, there is none blind like those who will not see. Jehovah weighs the spirits.

Commit thy works unto the Lord, and thy thoughts shall be established [Prov. 16:3].

The word *commit* is literally "roll." You just roll your affairs over upon the Lord, and He will take charge. That's actually the way I got saved. When I was a lad, I ran away to Detroit, got into sin, came home, and was troubled by my conscience. Then a preacher told me that God wasn't angry at me—that Jesus bore my sins and that being justified by faith I could have peace with God. At that time I just rolled my sins onto Christ. There are times, even to this day, when I can't sleep at night, that I like to just roll over in bed and say, "Lord Jesus, I am resting in You." Roll over. Rest in Him. Commit thy works unto Jehovah.

Are you worried about tomorrow, next week, next year, or the unforeseeable future? How is it all going to work out? Why don't you just turn it over to Him? Roll it over onto Him. What a picture this is!

The Lord hath made all things for himself: yea, even the wicked for the day of evil [Prov. 16:4].

My friend, here is some strong medicine. This proverb is a pill that will send you on a trip, I mean a real mind-blowing trip. Jehovah hath made all things for Himself. Have you ever wondered why the ocean is salty, or why it has a tide? You may answer that it is according to certain laws of nature. But who made the laws? Why is the ocean salty?

Because God wanted it that way! The Lord Jesus is the Creator, and He *wanted* it that way. Someone may say it is because there is salt in the land that has been filtered out by the water in the ocean. By the way, who put the salt in the land to begin with?

I don't care what you do with evolution or how far back you try to carry it, eventually you come to the place where somebody had to make something to get the whole thing *started*. You know who started it? God did. And not only that, He made all these things for Himself.

What is the chief end of man? I learned that in the catechism a long time ago, and the answer is good. The chief end of man is to glorify God and to enjoy Him forever. I don't care who you are or where you are, God created you for His glory. Somebody says, "What about the drunkard in the street? What about that crooked man? That lost man—what about him? You mean he's for the glory of God?" My friend, this is a strong pill—are you ready to swallow it? *All of that is for the glory of God.* "Oh," you may say, "I don't like that." I don't remember that God ever asked anyone whether or not he liked it. He has never asked me that.

Very frankly, there are certain things that I don't understand, and I think I could make some very fine suggestions to the Lord. But the Lord says, "Vernon McGee, I didn't make this universe for you. This universe exists for Me, and you exist for Me; and you are going to be for My glory whether you are good or bad, saved or lost." God is accomplishing *His* purpose today. Don't you think it is about time you got in step with God? He is the One running the thing.

So many people want to make sure that they are going with the crowd, going with the thing that is popular, going with the thing that will work out. Friend, I don't know how things are going to work out in this world, but I do know this: Ultimately it's all going to be for the glory of God. "Even the lawless for the day of evil." God is going to make the wrath of man to praise Him (Ps. 76:10). How is He going to do that? I don't know. Let's wait—He will show us someday. Are you willing to trust Him and commit your way to Him and get in step with Him?

The very wonderful thing is that God is moving this universe according to His plan and purpose. The Greeks had a proverb: "The dice of the gods are loaded." That is exactly what God is saying in this proverb. Whether you like it or don't like it, God is saying to you, "Don't gamble with Me. Don't act as if I don't exist. You can play house as if I don't exist, as if this is your universe and you are going to work it out your way. But I want you to know that if you start gambling with Me, you will lose. You see, this is My universe, and I make the dice to come up My way, not your way. My dice are loaded—I already know how they are coming up, and you don't." The thing for us to do is to get in step with God.

A man, the Scriptures say, is a fool to live without God. "The fool hath said in his heart, There is no God . . ." (Ps. 14:1). ". . . he that cometh to God must believe that he is, and that he is a rewarder of them that diligently seek him" (Heb. 11:6).

This is a pill, is it not? And it is one that is hard for men to swallow.

When a man's ways please the LORD, he maketh even his enemies to be at peace with him [Prov. 16:7].

I have wrestled with this proverb a great deal, and I have searched what other men have had to say on this. Do you mean to tell me that if your ways please Jehovah, you will not have an enemy? Well, if that were true, then God wouldn't have an enemy, and He *does* have an enemy.

My interpretation is that if your ways please Jehovah, then your enemy may hate you; and, by the way, he *will* hate you. But the interesting thing is that, when the chips are down, these folk will admit that God is using you. That's the important thing. One of the nicest things that has been said about me in Southern California was said by a man who very frankly says he hates me. He said, "I hate him, but he teaches the Word of God." I say, "Thank you, Mr. Enemy, you are carrying out this proverb. You have to make that kind of acknowledgment if you're honest." I love this proverb, by the way.

A just weight and balance are the LORD's: all the weights of the bag are his work [Prov. 16:11].

This is a word for the butcher, the baker, and the candlestick maker.

Pride goeth before destruction, and an haughty spirit before a fall [Prov. 16:18].

I have that underlined in my Bible.

Better it is to be of an humble spirit with the lowly, than to divide the spoil with the proud [Prov. 16:19].

Here again is a thrust made against that which God hates—pride. Pride is number one on God's "hate parade" (Prov. 6:16–19). This is the thing that brought down the archangel whom we know as Satan today. He was Lucifer—son of the morning—probably the highest creature God created until sin was found in him. What was that sin? It was pride: he attempted to lift himself above God, because he was such a great creature whom God had created and given the power of free choice.

Free choice is a very dangerous weapon which God has put in the hands of some of His creatures. Now some creatures follow an instinct. For example, the ducks leave Canada in the wintertime and fly down to South America. In the summer they fly back up to Canada. Back and forth they go. They are moved by instinct, but man has a free will. Man can stay in Canada in the wintertime (I don't know why he would), and he can go south in the summertime. But where there is free choice, there is also the possibility of pride and rebellion against God.

There are so many in Scripture who illustrate this matter of pride. This is the thing that was the undoing of that man Haman in the Book of Esther. And Absalom—imagine him rebelling against his father, David! Goliath, the giant, boasted in his pride. And Ahab was filled with pride.

Pleasant words are as an honeycomb, sweet to the soul, and health to the bones [Prov. 16:24].

"Pleasant words." We all like to hear something good, don't we? We read the newspaper and always get the bad news. It's too bad more people don't read the Bible. It is filled with good news. That is what the gospel is—*good* news.

Also, we should learn to say it with pleasant words *now*—instead of trying to say it with flowers when it is too late.

> **There is a way that seemeth right unto a man, but the end thereof are the ways of death [Prov. 16:25].**

You will recognize that we had this proverb before (Prov. 14:12). Then why is it repeated? It is because the Lord doesn't want us to miss this one. Repetition reveals its importance.

> **An ungodly man diggeth up evil: and in his lips there is as a burning fire [Prov. 16:27].**

We probably all know someone who fits this proverb. I had a friend who professed to be a Christian, but almost every time I would see him he would start in, "Dr. McGee, have you heard . . . ?" Then he would go on with the latest and the juiciest gossip that was going around. Was he a godly man? I don't know. I cannot sit in judgment on him. We need to guard our own tongue and lips so that we do not do the same.

> **A froward man soweth strife: and a whisperer sepa-rateth chief friends [Prov. 16:28].**

We said before that some people will believe anything if it is whis-pered to them. There are those people who go around and whisper things—separating friends.

> **The hoary head is a crown of glory, if it be found in the way of righteousness [Prov. 16:31].**

This is a good motto for the senior citizen.

**The lot is cast into the lap; but the whole disposing
thereof is of the LORD [Prov. 16:33].**

I have this verse written over the Book of Esther. In his pride Haman
cast lots to determine the day of destruction of the Jewish people. But
God intervened and delivered His people; and the Jewish Feast of Pu-
rim (meaning "lots") is a celebration of that providential day.

Let me say again that "the dice of the gods are loaded." Don't gamble with God. Don't take a chance with Him. Remember that it is
God's universe, and it is all for His glory. It's for His purpose. Do you
want to cooperate? Do you want to get in step with God or continue in
rebellion? It is not your will, but God's will that shall prevail. Oh, that
you and I would get in step with Him and be at peace with Him, being
justified by faith!

CHAPTER 17

Better is a dry morsel, and quietness therewith, than an house full of sacrifices with strife [Prov. 17:1].

This verse is very similar in thought to Proverbs 15:17: "Better is a dinner of herbs where love is, than a stalled ox and hatred therewith." The last part of the verse pictures a scene of religious activity, but activity does not always denote the working of God. A church can have a lot of meetings, a lot of organization, and a tremendous amount of activity, but all of this may cause a great deal of confusion and frustration.

I think of Elijah in the court of Ahab and Jezebel. There certainly was plenty of activity going on in Ahab's palace, including a lot of religious practices, but nothing really pertaining to God. Elijah stepped in and proclaimed that it wasn't going to rain until God said so, and He wasn't in the mood to say so. Then Elijah walked out. Where did he go? He went far off to the Brook Cherith where he stayed a long time alone with God. God was training him out in the quietness of the desert. "Better is a dry morsel, and quietness therewith."

God took Moses out of the palace of Pharaoh (another scene of great activity and religious organization) and put him in the desert of Midian and taught him there. Both Moses and Elijah had "a dry morsel, and quietness therewith."

It is nice to get off at times and be by yourself. My wife and I are busy at many conferences, and we have had to cut down on the number of them in order to get some quietness and rest. When we get home from a series of conferences, we go nowhere but just outside on our patio. I tell my wife, "Come on out here, and let's sit down together and get acquainted with each other. I've been married to you a long time, and it's time I was getting acquainted with you." It's a good thing for us to do. God wants us to have times like that. They are very important for our spiritual refreshment.

> **A wise servant shall have rule over a son that causeth shame, and shall have part of the inheritance among the brethren [Prov. 17:2].**

A servant who is faithful is better than a son who is not faithful. It is better to have a servant in whom you can have confidence than a son you cannot trust.

I think here of Abraham and his faithful servant Eliezer, and of David and his son Absalom. Abraham told the Lord that Eliezer was his only heir and that he wanted a son (Gen. 15:2). He felt it was much better to have a son, and God answered his request. But if the son is not dependable, if he is going to be like David's son Absalom, who openly rebelled against him, then certainly it is much better to have a good, faithful servant. And David had a number of faithful men who stayed right with him.

> **The fining pot is for silver, and the furnace for gold: but the Lord trieth the hearts [Prov. 17:3].**

To get pure silver, the mined ore must be put into the fining pot and heated until it melts so that the dross can be removed and the pure metal remain. The same thing applies to gold; it is put in the furnace, and the dross is drawn off. And the Lord puts His servants into the fire so that He can develop something in them. He tries our hearts in order to strengthen us. He wants to produce better sons and daughters for His use.

We are more precious to God than gold or silver. Therefore, we should not be discouraged when we are tested. "Wherein ye greatly rejoice, though now for a season, if need be, ye are in heaviness through manifold temptations: that the trial of your faith, being much more precious than of gold that perisheth, though it be tried with fire, might be found unto praise and honour and glory at the appearing of Jesus Christ" (1 Pet. 1:6–7). God uses this method.

God had a purpose in allowing Job to go through the furnace of affliction. God had a purpose in giving Paul a thorn in the flesh. God had a purpose in permitting the period of martyrdom that came to the church. Persecution actually molded the church, and it has never been as rich spiritually as it was during that period.

I think one of the problems among Christians today is our affluence. This was one of the problems in Israel. Moses described it in Deuteronomy 32:15: "But Jeshurun waxed fat, and kicked: thou art waxen fat, thou art grown thick, thou art covered with fatness; then he forsook God which made him, and lightly esteemed the Rock of his salvation." I'm afraid we may have a lot of fat saints today. They have everything, and yet they become complainers, faultfinders, critics. They really are no help to the cause of Christ. So God must put the saints that He is going to use into the furnace in order that He might develop them for His use.

I received a letter from a lady who prayed that she might know the Lord Jesus better, that she might grow in grace and the knowledge of Him. What did the Lord do? He gave her cancer. Someone might say, "That's no way for God to do." But that is the way He sometimes does it, friend. You are listening to a preacher who knows all about it. I know why God gave me cancer. One mean letter sent to my wife and me said that God gave us cancer because we won't obey God and we're ignorant, and because of the kind of folk we are. Well, some of that may be true. But He didn't do it in a mean spirit, the way the letter was written. He did not do it because He hates us or because He is mean. God did it in a loving way, and you don't know how precious He has become to us because of it.

Children's children are the crown of old men; and the glory of children are their fathers [Prov. 17:6].

Here is a verse I am sure many of you can appreciate. "Children's children" are grandchildren. It is a verse for grandfathers. "The glory of children are their fathers." Children look to their fathers. I have always been grateful for a daughter who has loved and respected her father. We have always been able to communicate, even though she has the same kind of temper that I have—a short fuse. Every now and then we have a blowup, but then I go to her or sometimes she comes to me. We don't even let the sun go down on our disagreement. But "children's children are the crown of old men." The proverb is right. Now I am an old man with grandsons, and I could bore you to tears talking about them. Perhaps you have heard of one old man saying to another old man, "Have I ever told you about my grandson and shown you pictures of him?" The other man replied, "No, you haven't, and I want to thank you for it!" If I had known how wonderful grandchildren can be, I would have had them before I had my children! They are a pride and joy to have around, and they draw families together. The child looks to the father, but the grandfather looks back to the grandchild; that is where his affection centers.

A reproof entereth more into a wise man than an hundred stripes into a fool [Prov. 17:10].

Somebody says, "You know, poor Mr. So-and-So, he's a wonderful child of God, and look at the trouble he has had!" God reproves his saints, sometimes by sending trouble into their lives. God is coaching them, because they are wise men. The wise man will listen to reproof.

The fool won't listen to reproof. Even if God laid a hundred stripes on his back, it wouldn't do him any good. When you see someone prospering who is ungodly, the reason may be that he is such a fool that no matter what God would do to him, he would not change. The Lord Jesus told about the man who took down his old barns to build new barns for his crops. He was prosperous and was expanding his business. There is nothing wrong with building a new barn. The thing wrong was that the man was a fool. I didn't say that—Jesus said it. He was a fool because he did nothing about eternity. The chastening of the Lord would not have changed him. During the Great Tribulation the world will go through such intense suffering and judgment that people will gnaw their own tongue. But do you think they will turn to God? No. A hundred stripes will not do any good when they are applied to a fool.

This leads me to repeat that I believe we have a wrong philosophy about prisons today. A prison is not for the purpose of developing men and putting them back into society. There may be some place for that, but a prison is primarily a place of punishment, not an institution for discipline. Discipline is for a child—your own child. Punishment is for the one who has committed a crime.

Wherefore is there a price in the hand of a fool to get wisdom, seeing he hath no heart to it? [Prov. 17:16].

I have known a lot of boys from wealthy families who had no heart for college at all. They shouldn't have been in college. It wasn't that they were not able to pass the courses, but they didn't want to go to college in the first place. Their hearts were not in it.

I do not agree with the philosophy that every person should have a college education. I think that every person should have access to a college education, but I do not think that young folks should be forced to go to college. A lot of young people don't have a capacity for it, nor do they have the heart for it. This has nothing to do with being rich or poor. It involves the desire to learn. I believe that every poor boy who really wants to learn should have the opportunity. The door ought to be opened for him. On the other hand, there are a lot of rich boys who should not be in college at all. I was a poor boy, and I thank God for a wonderful Christian elder who took an interest in me. If it hadn't been for that man, I could never have gone to college. I thank God for opening the door to college for this poor boy.

A friend loveth at all times, and a brother is born for adversity [Prov. 17:17].

This verse reminds us of Jonathan who was such a wonderful friend to David. "A friend loveth at *all* times." Jonathan loved David when he was playing his music in the palace as well as when he was hiding for his life, trying to escape King Saul. Although Jonathan was the son of Saul and heir to the throne, he loved David.

It is a wonderful thing to have a friend like that. If someone doesn't love you at *all* times, that person is not your friend. It is one of the disappointments of life to have someone profess to love you and be your friend, then when the chips are down, you find that he really does not love you after all. He was a Judas Iscariot or an Absalom, who betrayed you.

> **He that begetteth a fool doeth it to his sorrow: and the father of a fool hath no joy [Prov. 17:21].**

This has been repeated several times in Proverbs. The father of a son who is making good is a father full of joy. He will talk constantly about his boy. If he has a son who is not doing well, he becomes very silent, and no one hears about the boy.

> **A merry heart doeth good like a medicine: but a broken spirit drieth the bones [Prov. 17:22].**

There are a lot of folk today who are actually sick with a heart sickness. It is not heart trouble. It is a heart sickness, a lack of joy. They live down in Mudville. They are the mighty Casey who struck out at bat. This description applies to many Christians.

God wants us to have a merry heart. He wants us to have a big time! Our fellowship at church should be a place of fun. We should laugh and rejoice and praise God when we go to church. We are simply too stiff and stilted in our churches.

> **A wicked man taketh a gift out of the bosom to pervert the ways of judgment [Prov. 17:23].**

There are many different ways of bribing, and there is so much bribing going on in our world today.

> **Even a fool, when he holdeth his peace, is counted wise: and he that shutteth his lips is esteemed a man of understanding [Prov. 17:28].**

This proverb has humor in it. It says that it pays to keep your mouth shut.

An Arkansas farmer had a son who was simple. Folks would say he was "not all there." They drove into town with a load of apples, and the father left the son to sit and hold the reins of the horses while he went off on an errand. "Now, son," said the father, "don't you say anything to anybody because if you do, they will find out you are a fool." The boy promised he wouldn't open his mouth. A man came up to the wagon and asked, "How much are your apples, son?" The boy never said a word. The man asked two or three times, but the boy just sat there and looked at him. Finally the man said, "What in the world is wrong? You act like a fool." Then he walked away. When the father returned, he asked the boy, "How did things go?" The boy answered, "I kept my mouth shut, but they found out I was a fool anyway."

CHAPTER 18

O ur young man who has entered the school of wisdom is progress-
ing. I hope the rest of us are coming along with him and are
learning the spiritual truths that are in these proverbs.

**Through desire a man, having separated himself,
seeketh and intermeddleth with all wisdom [Prov.
18:1].**

Let me give a translation which I think will be helpful: "A man having separated himself for his own pleasure rageth against all sound
wisdom." The important thing here is the subject of separation, and
this is the wrong kind of separation.

The great division in the human family is between saved people
and lost people. That is the division that God sees. He does not make
divisions like we do into categories of black, white, yellow, or red.
God is really "color-blind." Now the Bible does teach a separation of
the saved people from the lost people: "Wherefore come out from
among them, and be ye separate, saith the Lord, and touch not the
unclean thing; and I will receive you" (2 Cor. 6:17). God makes it very
clear that His people are to separate themselves from that which is
unclean. He is referring particularly to the idolatry, the immorality,
and the filthy conversation of the unsaved. There should be a separation from that. By the way, this is real segregation: segregate yourself
from the evil. That is important to do. There are many saved folk who
emphasize separation. They form cliques and groups and practice the
wrong kind of separation. They make up their own little commandments, which are not actually in the Bible. They follow them and feel
that they should separate themselves from other believers, and they
feel that this makes them very special people in the sight of the Lord.
They think they are superior. Generally they are not. They manifest

many evidences of the flesh working in their lives. That is a wrong kind of separation.

There is another group of strong separationists, and they are among the unsaved. We find that this is what is referred to in this proverb. This is the person who has separated himself for his own pleasure. He refuses to listen to anything that is wise. Jude speaks of them as being apostates and says this: "These be they who separate themselves, sensual, having not the Spirit" (Jude 19). They withdraw themselves from any group or individual who might reprimand them and begin their own little group and become very obnoxious. Generally they are apostates: they separate themselves from the truth. They certainly cause a great deal of sorrow in this world.

A fool hath no delight in understanding, but that his heart may discover itself [Prov. 18:2].

A professor sent me a collection of modern proverbs. Some of them fit the proverbs we are studying from the Bible. This is one that possibly fits here: "If I stop to think before I speak, I won't have to worry afterward about what I said before." That certainly is true.

When the wicked cometh, then cometh also contempt, and with ignominy reproach [Prov. 18:3].

Another modern proverb is: "Some persons cause happiness wherever they go; others, *whenever* they go." I think that is a good one and would apply to the crowd mentioned in this verse. These are some people who also bring great sorrow into the world.

The words of a man's mouth are as deep waters, and the wellspring of wisdom as a flowing brook [Prov. 18:4].

Every true believer in the Lord Jesus Christ is indwelt by the Holy Spirit. The Lord Jesus stood in the temple when the water was poured out at the time of the Feast of Tabernacles and said, ". . . If any man thirst, let him come unto me, and drink. He that believeth on me, as the scripture hath said, out of his belly [inmost being] shall flow rivers of living water" (John 7:37-38). Then John interprets this for us. "(But this spake he of the Spirit, which they that believe on him should receive: for the Holy Ghost was not yet given; because that Jesus was not yet glorified.)" (John 7:39). The child of God should learn to speak in the power of the Holy Spirit. This is so important in presenting the Word of God and talking about the things of God.

> **It is not good to accept the person of the wicked, to overthrow the righteous in judgment [Prov. 18:5].**

Do not compromise with an evil person or a lawless person in order to overthrow a righteous person. This applies to individuals. I believe it also applies to nations. I wonder if perhaps our nation has been guilty of compromising with wicked nations. We have interfered in too many places, and we have gotten ourselves into serious difficulties. These proverbs are practical, and they can be geared right into life.

> **A fool's lips enter into contention, and his mouth calleth for strokes.**
>
> **A fool's mouth is his destruction, and his lips are the snare of his soul.**
>
> **The words of a talebearer are as wounds, and they go down into the innermost parts of the belly [Prov. 18:6-8].**

"The words of a talebearer" or the words of a *whisperer* are as dainty morsels that go down into the depth of the soul. We are back again to the subject of the fool. Remember that the Lord Jesus has told us that we are not to call anyone a fool (see Matt. 5:22). However, God calls some people fools because He knows them.

We find again that the fool is a source of trouble. He is the one who is always stirring up contention, issuing complaints, finding fault.

We can give another fitting modern proverb: "Be considerate. Most people know how to express a complaint, but few utter a gracious compliment. The bee is seldom complimented for making honey; it is just criticized for stinging." How true!

The name of the LORD is a strong tower: the righteous runneth into it, and is safe [Prov. 18:10].

The name of Jehovah is also the name of the Lord Jesus Christ. He is called Jesus because He saves His people from their sins. And He is called Christ because He is the Anointed One. He is the Lord of our life and our salvation! The Lord is a strong tower. You can run into it and be completely safe. This is a verse that many have used in speaking to children, and I have used it myself and found it very effective. It speaks of security and reminds us that no one can pluck us out of His hands. What a beautiful picture this is!

The rich man's wealth is his strong city, and as an high wall in his own conceit [Prov. 18:11].

There are basic differences between Israel and the church which we need to recognize. Material wealth was one of the promises of God to His people Israel, but He did not promise that to us. God promised them a full basket, and He made good His word. He also said He would take away their wealth as a judgment. The church is not a continuation of Israel even though that is sometimes preached today. The church is not the next grade above Judaism. You can make a comparison, of course, and there are many likenesses. The contrasts, however, are greater. The church has not been promised material blessings. God has blessed us as believers ". . . with all *spiritual* blessings in heavenly places in Christ" (Eph. 1:3, italics mine). The child of God needs to be fortified. He needs to get into the strong tower. He needs to be in this strong city and have the high wall around him. What is it? Well, it is a knowledge of the Word of God. We need to recognize that we are living in very difficult times and we are being tested. Oh, how important is a knowledge of the Word of God! My friend, don't try to substitute these little courses that teach you how to witness and how to get along with your wife. They may have a certain value, but they are only surface stuff. There is no substitute for digging into the Word of God. My friend, learn to read the Word of God. If you don't understand it, read it again. If you don't understand it the second time, go over it once more. Then if you don't understand it the third time through, something is wrong, and you need to go to the Lord and tell Him you're not getting it. Ask Him to help you. The Spirit of God is our teacher. I know I am telling you this accurately because He hasn't yet let me down in this matter of understanding His Word.

He that answereth a matter before he heareth it, it is folly and shame unto him [Prov. 18:13].

How often people try to pass judgment on someone else when they don't really know the person or the problem or the situation under which that person lives. How important it is to have all the facts before we express an opinion!

The spirit of a man will sustain his infirmity; but a wounded spirit who can bear? [Prov. 18:14].

You can break your leg and recover from that; but, if your spirit is broken, you are completely broken. Only God can encourage you at a time like that. Remember at the time of Nehemiah's governorship over the people of Israel, and even after they had rebuilt the walls, they still had not heard the Word of God. When the Word of God was read to them, they saw how far they were from God and they began to weep. Nehemiah told them not to weep because it was a time of rejoicing. He said, ". . . the joy of the LORD is your strength" (Neh. 8:10). How important is it for us to know that the joy of the Lord is our strength. Sitting in the pastor's study of a church in Salem, Oregon, I noticed this little motto (it's a contemporary proverb) on the wall: "Joy is the flag that is flown in the heart when the Master is in residence." I like that. When the Lord Jesus Christ becomes first choice in your life, when He has top priority, then you will not have that broken spirit that we hear so much about today. Give God the first choice. Give of your time, your effort, your thoughts, your companionship, and your money, and see what happens. Have you tried that?

> **A man's gift maketh room for him, and bringeth him before great men [Prov. 18:16].**

I hope you will nail this one down. Some critics have compared this verse with Proverbs 25:14 and have pointed it out as an apparent contradiction in the Bible; however, when we get to that chapter, we will find out that it is a contrast and not a contradiction at all.

This verse speaks of gifts, and as I have mentioned before, I believe every believer in Christ has a gift. *Gifts of the Spirit* is a message we have in print that develops this subject.

> **Death and life are in the power of the tongue: and they that love it shall eat the fruit thereof [Prov. 18:21].**

"Death and life are in the power of the tongue"—think of that! Your tongue can be used to give out the gospel, and this will give life. It can also be used to say things that would drive people away from God, which makes it an instrument of death. The little tongue is the most potent weapon in this world. The Bible has much to say about the tongue, and we find a lot about it in the Book of Proverbs.

> **Whoso findeth a wife findeth a good thing, and obtaineth favour of the LORD [Prov. 18:22].**

I have actually laughed at the thought that these two verses are side by side in the Word of God. The Spirit of God put them together. The tongue is used when the fellow proposes to the girl. He asks her to marry him, and that is the proper way for it to be done; and death and life are in the power of the tongue. You may wish you had bitten off your tongue before you asked the fatal question. It's like the story of the old bachelor who had never met a woman whom he wanted to marry because he thought they all talked too much. He found what we used to call an old maid, one who seemed very quiet. He fell in love with her and asked her to marry him. The minute she accepted the proposal, she started talking. She talked about where they would go and how they would fix their house and on and on. Suddenly after an hour or so she realized that she was doing all the talking and that he was quiet. "Why don't you say something?" she asked. He answered, "I've said too much already!"

"Whoso findeth a wife findeth a good thing, and obtaineth favour of the LORD." I want to say that I have always thanked the Lord for my wife. It is wonderful to have a good wife—and to have someone who is able to put up with me!

> **A man that hath friends must shew himself friendly: and there is a friend that sticketh closer than a brother [Prov. 18:24].**

If you want to have friends, then show yourself friendly. By the way, are you a friend to your friends?

"There is a friend that sticketh closer than a brother." Do you know who He is? He is closer to you than a brother can be. Jesus is the One, and He says, "Ye are my friends, if ye do whatsoever I command you" (John 15:14). When I hear folk singing "Jesus is a Friend of Mine," I want to go up to them and ask, "Are you obeying His commands?" Jesus says, "Ye are my friends, if ye do whatsoever I command you." If you are not obeying Him, I take it that you're not one of His friends.

Jesus is a friend who will stick closer than a brother. He is our Savior. He loved us enough to die for us. He is the one who says, ". . . lo, I am with you alway, even unto the end of the world . . ." (Matt. 28:20) and ". . . I will never leave thee, nor forsake thee" (Heb. 13:5). Also He has given us this promise: "And if I go and prepare a place for you, I will come again, and receive you unto myself; that where I am, there ye may be also" (John 14:3). There isn't anything you can do to improve such an arrangement. We have a wonderful Friend who sticks closer than any brother.

CHAPTER 19

Better is the poor that walketh in his integrity, than he that is perverse in his lips, and is a fool [Prov. 19:1].

The Lord has forbidden us to call anyone a fool, but the Spirit of God has really been using that word. Apparently there are quite a few fools in the human family.

Also, that the soul be without knowledge, it is not good; and he that hasteth with his feet sinneth.

The foolishness of man perverteth his way: and his heart fretteth against the LORD [Prov. 19:2–3].

There is an antithetic parallelism all through these proverbs. Here is a contrast between those who are the children of God and those who are not. The one is in the path of truth; the other, who is in the path of self-will and ignorance, God calls a fool.

We have a modern proverb: "Where ignorance is bliss, 'tis folly to be wise." This is a false proverb. Sometimes people—even officers of the church—pride themselves on being ignorant of the Bible. In board meetings I have heard church officers speak out saying, "Well, that is theological; that is biblical, and I don't know much about that." I had to bite my lip from saying, *Why in the world don't you know it? You are a mature man, an officer in the church, and you should not be that devoid of spiritual understanding!*

Someone sent me this proverb: "No man is uneducated who knows the Bible, and no one is truly educated who is ignorant of its teachings." Although the world does not accept this, I believe it is true. I do not think a man can be truly educated if he is ignorant of the Bible. Certainly one cannot be a mature Christian and be ignorant of the Bible. A knowledge of the Word of God should be a characteristic of the child of God.

Wealth maketh many friends; but the poor is separated from his neighbour [Prov. 19:4].

Wealthy people seem to have a lot of friends. Their houses are full of guests so long as the refrigerator is filled and the bar is well stocked and there is music and entertainment.

It is interesting to note that the Word of God admonishes the child of God to seek out the poor man. You will remember that James, in a practical way, speaks of a man who comes into your assembly ". . . with a gold ring, in goodly apparel, and there come in also a poor man in vile raiment; and ye have respect to him that weareth the gay clothing, and say unto him, Sit thou here in a good place; and say to the poor, Stand thou there, or sit here under my footstool" (James 2:2–3).

Unfortunately, it is true that the poor man has his problems in many of our churches. A couple was telling me about their personal experience. They are poor and not able to buy the latest in style, and what they wear looks pretty worn. They went to a church that has a reputation of being a very conservative, evangelical church. My, they were snubbed. What happened to them is terrible!

Human nature has not changed down through the centuries. The old nature is still being revealed. My mother used to ask me before she went out, "Is my petticoat showing?" Now my wife asks me the same thing. There are a lot of folk who are stepping out, going to church, and moving in the society of their particular group whose *old nature* is showing. And it shows in matters like separating the poor from their society. God lays it on the line, doesn't He? "The poor is separated from his neighbour." When they find out you are a poor boy, they don't want you around.

A false witness shall not be unpunished, and he that speaketh lies shall not escape [Prov. 19:5].

Drop down to verse 9 and see that it is almost the same statement. "A false witness shall not be unpunished, and he that speaketh lies shall perish." A false witness is not going to "escape." He will be found out. He will be called to account for what he has said. Not only that, he is going to "perish." God tells us that in Revelation 21:8.

We think of Ahab and Jezebel in connection with the episode of Naboth's vineyard. The record is in 1 Kings 21 and 22. Because Naboth would not give up his vineyard to the king, arrangements were made to have false witnesses bring an untrue charge against him and then stone him to death. Ahab thought he got by with this crime, but Elijah met him and told him that where Naboth's innocent blood had been shed, the dogs would lick his blood. What happened was this: Ahab went into battle against Syria, with Jehoshaphat in alliance with him. He put Jehoshaphat out in front wearing his royal robes, but Ahab disguised himself as a common soldier to escape notice. But a trigger happy soldier on the enemy side "drew a bow at a venture"— he didn't even know who he was aiming at, but that old arrow had Ahab's name on it. When it went out from the bow with a zing it said, "Ahab, where are you? I'm looking for you." And it found him. He bled like a stuck pig, and he died. The blood ran out of the wound in the chariot, "And one washed the chariot in the pool of Samaria; and the dogs licked up his blood; and they washed his armour; according unto the word of the LORD which he spake" (1 Kings 22:38). You say that is crude and frightful. I agree. But, my friend, lying, false witnessing, and gossip in God's sight are really frightful, and God hates them. "A false witness shall not be unpunished, and he that speaketh lies shall not escape."

Many will entreat the favour of the prince: and every man is a friend to him that giveth gifts [Prov. 19:6].

"Many will entreat the favour of the prince"—we don't have a prince, but we write letters to our congressmen and our governor, and sometimes even to our president when we want legislation passed.

"Every man is a friend to him that giveth gifts." That is certainly true. A man will have plenty of friends as long as he is giving out gifts.

> **All the brethren of the poor do hate him: how much more do his friends go far from him? he pursueth them with words, yet they are wanting to him [Prov. 19:7].**

The brethren of the poor may not hate him as we think of hateful behavior. Often they just don't have anything to do with him. They ignore him. A prosperous man may see his ne'er-do-well brother drive up in an old jalopy, so he says to his wife, "Let's get into the bedroom and lock the door and make him think that we're not home." That is what it means to hate your brother. The poor don't do very well in this world, by the way.

We hear so much from the people who campaign for office about how they are going to help us poor folk. The only thing they ever help me with is more taxes. Every time we have an election my taxes go up. Every politician promises to give us some relief. No one has yet, and I don't think anyone will. My feeling is that the problems have mounted so that no man can solve them. No man, I don't care who he is, is able to solve the problems of the world today.

Do you know what we need? We need politicians to call us back to God. We need someone to say, "Look, I don't have the answer to the world's problems. Let's turn to God for the answer. Let's serve Him, let's pray to Him." Since we have tried everything else to solve our problems, wouldn't it be well for us to try God for a change? It would be far better for us to listen to God than to listen to so much television. We have heard everybody else and all their opinions on the talk shows. They have strutted across the stage of human events, and it hasn't been very impressive. We need to turn to God and listen to Him.

> **A foolish son is the calamity of his father: and the contentions of a wife are a continual dropping [Prov. 19:13].**

Our last proverb about this matter said that when a man finds a wife, he has found a good thing. That is, he finds the other half of him, and she is to be a helpmeet for him. She is not to be a servant. Where do people get the idea that the wife is to obey the husband? The wife is to submit herself to her husband provided he is the right kind of man. If he is not, I don't think God has asked her to submit herself. The only instructions I find about submission apply to the Christian home. A wife is to submit to a Christian husband who loves her just like Christ loves the church. When a woman has that kind of husband, she can submit herself to him.

This proverb almost makes one laugh even though it tells of a tragic situation. Think of the poor husband who has a foolish son and also has a wife who is contentious. You can imagine what kind of a home he lives in. That is why it is so wonderful to find the right kind of a wife.

> **House and riches are the inheritance of fathers: and a prudent wife is from the Lord [Prov. 19:14].**

If you have a good wife, you got her from the Lord. You ought to thank the Lord for her, by the way. Have you ever done that? Thank the Lord for your good wife, because He is the One who gave her to you.

Young men, this should tell you something. Do you want a good wife? The one who gives away good wives is not the father of the daughter. Many a father is glad to get rid of his daughter. But our Heavenly Father has a lot of good wives to give away. Keep in touch with Him, and He will lead you to the right one. He wants to give you the right kind of wife. This is a very practical proverb. Don't you agree?

> **Chasten thy son while there is hope, and let not thy soul spare for his crying [Prov. 19:18].**

Start with your discipline when the children are young. Don't wait until it is too late. A man who was saved later in life told me, "My wife and I were saved recently, and we are thanking God for it, but we have lost our children. We used to live like the devil, and we can see that in our children today." They had waited until too late to give their children the proper training.

Start when the children are young. Don't mind if little Willie cries when you paddle him. On the other hand, every father needs to be very careful in the way he deals with his child. No one has the right to be brutal in his dealings with his children. Dr. Ironside has translated the proverb this way: "Chasten thy son while there is hope, but set not thy soul upon slaying him." Don't be afraid to discipline, but a brutal punishment is not to be permitted. Brutality can only tear down the child and destroy his spirit. As a matter of fact, even the law of the land can, and should, step in whenever there is brutality to children.

God has given very definite commands for Christians. He tells children to obey their parents (Eph. 6:1). But then he says to the fathers, "And, ye fathers, provoke not your children to wrath . . ." (Eph. 6:4). Don't wade into them when you are angry. They know you are angry and that you are just venting your anger and frustration. At that time you will probably punish too hard—in fact, you can be brutal. The command is to bring them up in the ". . . nurture and admonition of the Lord" (Eph. 6:4), that is, the discipline and the instruction of the Lord.

There are many devices in a man's heart; nevertheless the counsel of the Lord, that shall stand [Prov. 19:21].

Man can come up with many explanations, many solutions, but God is the only One who can give you the right kind of advice. Many can make a computer, but only God can put sense into it.

The desire of a man is his kindness: and a poor man is better than a liar [Prov. 19:22].

This is a strange proverb, isn't it? "The desire [or charm] of a man is his kindness." How many folk do you know like that? They are kind, generous, lovely people. Then we are brought back to the poor man, the poor relative, who comes for dinner and stays for a couple of years to live with you. Well, it is better to have him than to have a liar.

The fear of the LORD tendeth to life: and he that hath it shall abide satisfied; he shall not be visited with evil [Prov. 19:23].

The fear of the Lord does not mean that you are cringing, constantly in dread, living a life of terror. This proverb makes it clear that the real fear of God means that you can rest satisfied. It means that you recognize Him, you have looked to Him, you have accepted Him, and you want to follow Him. Now you can rest satisfied.

A slothful man hideth his hand in his bosom, and will not so much as bring it to his mouth again [Prov. 19:24].

An alternate translation is: "A slothful man burieth his hand in the dish." Here is another proverb that is humorous. This man is so lazy that he can put his hand down into the dish to eat, but he is too lazy to bring it back up to his mouth. When you get to that place, you're lazy! Unfortunately, we often see this in the spiritual realm. The Word of God is our food. I know Christians who will hold the Bible in their hands but are too lazy to read it.

Judgments are prepared for scorners, and stripes for the back of fools [Prov. 19:29].

Judgment is coming—that is quite obvious. God is not soft on the guilty. The pleasures of sin are for a season, but the wages of sin last for all eternity.

CHAPTER 20

We are still in this long section which sets before us the wisdom of Solomon. It is specifically directed to young men but actually applies to every Christian. In fact, the unbelievers can learn a great deal from these proverbs. The reading and study of the Word of God will have a definite effect upon the life of anyone. It will either bring you to God or it will drive you from Him. Your reaction to the Word of God cannot be neutral.

This is the first time there is a warning concerning alcohol or booze—I like the word *booze* because it has all the connotation of the evil that liquor has done down through the ages. I suppose that alcohol has wrecked more nations, more businesses, more homes, more individual lives than any other single factor.

Wine is a mocker, strong drink is raging: and whosoever is deceived thereby is not wise [Prov. 20:1].

There has always been a controversy about the "wine" in the New Testament being an intoxicant. It is my firm conviction that the Lord Jesus did not make an intoxicating drink at the wedding in Cana of Galilee (see John 2). Anyone who attempts to make of Him a bootlegger is ridiculous and is doing absolutely an injustice. Folk like to present the argument that in the warm climate of Israel all one had to do was to put grape juice in a wine skin and in time it would ferment. Yes, but in the miracle at Cana, the Lord Jesus started out with *water*, and in the matter of a few seconds He had "wine." My friend, it didn't have a chance to ferment. And we must remember that the wedding in Cana was a religious service, and everything that had to do with leaven (which is fermentation) was forbidden. This is the reason that at the time of the Passover and the institution of the Lord's Supper the wine could not have been fermented. Fermentation is the working of leaven, and leaven was strictly forbidden in bread and in everything else. The bread and drink could not have been leavened. Intoxicants are condemned in the Word of God, and here is a verse for it: "Wine is a mocker, strong drink is raging: and whosoever is deceived thereby is not wise."

Today many folk are being trapped by this type of thing. America is becoming a nation of drunkards. I am not impressed when the news media lets us know the tremendous amount of taxes that comes from the liquor industry. What they forget to tell is the cost of the hospitals, the mental institutions and the accidents—the people who have been maimed for life—as a result of drinking drivers. That kind of cost is not reported. I understand that any derogatory news is supressed because one of the biggest advertisers is the booze industry. We hear about how bad drug abuse is today; but remember, alcohol is a drug!

A law enforcement officer told me that at the beginning of the drug craze the liquor interests helped to fight the drug traffic, because they were afraid it would hurt their business. They would much rather have a kid become a drunkard addicted to alcohol than to have him become a drug addict. That is really generous and big-hearted of the liquor industry, don't you agree? However, young people began making comparisons. I have had young folk in youth groups tell me they don't feel they should be reprimanded for smoking marijuana by a crowd that sits around drinking cocktails. And I agree with the young folk. Let the adults stop drinking liquor before they talk to our young people about the evils of marijuana. The hypocrisy of those outside the church is lots worse than the hypocrisy inside the church!

Drunkenness was the undoing of Noah, and it has been a problem from that day to the present hour. Alcohol is valuable for medicinal purposes, but the minute it is used as a beverage it becomes dangerous. The number of alcoholics is increasing every year. It is one of the greatest tax burdens we have to bear. But you don't learn of that through the news media. In fact, it is dangerous to lift your head against this hydra-headed monster. I predict that it will not be missiles but liquor that will destroy our nation.

It is an honour for a man to cease from strife: but every fool will be meddling [Prov. 20:3].

One of the marks of a Christian should be that he does not prolong tension and strife. Someone has said that the only persons we should try to "get even with" are the people who have helped us. In other words, repay good with good. But don't try to get even with your enemies. Do not respond with evil for evil. Instead, be yielded to God, for God has said, ". . . Vengeance is mine; I will repay, saith the Lord" (Rom. 12:19). It is on that basis that God tells us not to avenge ourselves. It is actually a departure from the pathway of faith to attempt to take matters into our own hands. God can do it lots better than we can.

The child of God should remember what Paul said to the Philippian believers: "Let your moderation be known unto all men. The Lord is at hand" (Phil. 4:5). Matthew Arnold translated *moderation* as "sweet reasonableness." "Let your sweet reasonableness be known unto all men." That is the meaning of the proverb—"It is an honour for a man to cease from strife." How important it is!

The sluggard will not plow by reason of the cold; therefore shall he beg in harvest, and have nothing [Prov. 20:4].

Israel has a moderate climate, and winter is the season for preparing the soil for the spring planting. The sluggard, the lazy oaf, would say it was too cold, so he would stay by the fire. He would say he'll wait until it gets warmer. The problem would be that when it got warmer it was already too late to plow. That would be the time to be doing the planting. There is a note of humor in this verse.

It reminds me of the man whose house had a leaky roof. The reason he didn't fix it was because he didn't want to work on it when it was raining, and when it wasn't raining it didn't need fixing.

We come now to a set of proverbs that at first seem totally unrelated. However, there does appear to be a relationship based on words that speak of goodness or moral principles.

> **Most men will proclaim every one his own goodness:
> but a faithful man who can find? [Prov. 20:6].**

The theme here is "goodness."

> **The just man walketh in his integrity: his children are
> blessed after him [Prov. 20:7].**

The word here is "integrity."

> **A king that sitteth in the throne of judgment scattereth
> away all evil with his eyes [Prov. 20:8].**

"Scattering away all evil" is cleaning up his kingdom.

> **Who can say, I have made my heart clean, I am pure
> from my sin? [Prov. 20:9].**

The words here are "clean" and "pure."

> **Divers weights, and divers measures, both of them are
> alike abomination to the LORD [Prov. 20:10].**

Falseness is contrasted to goodness.

> **Even a child is known by his doings, whether his work
> be pure, and whether it be right [Prov. 20:11].**

The emphasis here is upon goodness even in children.

> **The hearing ear, and the seeing eye, the LORD hath made
> even both of them [Prov. 20:12].**

The thought here is to use your head. God has given you ears, and He
has given you eyes. Look and listen—that is not only good advice be-

fore you cross a railroad track, it is good when you are facing life every day.

All the way through this group of proverbs we see two great principles. First of all, "Who can say, I have made my heart clean, I am pure from my sin?" Well, can you, my friend? I am sure that neither you nor I can say that. No man by his own efforts can claim to be pure. Even the little baby in the crib cannot claim that. Those little ones reveal temper while they are still infants. At first my little grandson seemed to me to be free from sin. He was so wonderful! Then I found that he had a temper—he would get red in the face and even hold his breath! I had to realize that he was subject to the total depravity of man like the rest of us. Of course I told my wife, "I believe he's beginning to show some of the characteristics of his grandmother!" No man in his natural state can say, "I have made my heart clean, I am pure from my sin." My friend, if you would be heaven *bound,* you must first be heaven *born.* ". . . Verily, verily, I say unto thee, Except a man be born again, he cannot see the kingdom of God" (John 3:3). The Lord Jesus said that to a religious man, a good man. No man can call himself good or pure or right or clean until he has come to Christ for salvation and been clothed in the righteousness of Christ. Then he is accepted in the Beloved. But there is still that old nature that will stay with us until we enter into glory.

But notice from the proverbs that goodness does count, integrity does matter to God. Purity is worth something. A child of God should be walking in a way which commends the gospel of the grace of God.

Here is a good question which I have heard asked for many years: If you were arrested for being a Christian, would there be enough evidence to convict you? Suppose you were brought before a court on the accusation, "This fellow is a Christian." Would there be enough evidence there to convict you? Or would you be able to get off free? Would they look at your life and find you are not living like a Christian should? Would they find you do not walk in integrity? Would they find no goodness, no desire for purity?

The second thought in these proverbs is this: God has given you eyes to see and ears to hear. Use them. Stop, look, listen. Don't go blindly through life, seeing but not seeing. Use your eyes. Open your ears. God has given you a certain amount of common sense, a certain amount of "gumption." Listen to the news God has for you. You cannot make yourself pure. Only God can make you pure. God can give you a standing before Him that removes all the guilt of your sin and enables you to walk in integrity in this world.

> **Love not sleep, lest thou come to poverty; open thine eyes, and thou shalt be satisfied with bread [Prov. 20:13].**

He is saying, "Go to work." You will remember this is the same thing that Paul wrote to the Thessalonians. He said that if a man doesn't want to work, neither should he eat (see 2 Thess. 3:10). Those people were so excited about the possibility of the Lord's return that they were just waiting for the Lord. It is wonderful to be looking for Him and waiting for Him. But that doesn't mean that just sitting down and gazing into space is the way to wait for Him. A true anticipation of the coming of the Lord will cause a person to put his nose to the grindstone and work harder than ever before.

> **It is nought, it is nought, saith the buyer: but when he is gone his way, then he boasteth [Prov. 20:14].**

This is a humorous one, and I hope you can see the humor in it. A fellow goes in to buy an automobile, for example. He says to the man who is selling it, "I don't think this car is worth buying. The tires are almost worn out. The motor doesn't sound too good. There's a rattle back there. But I'll give you so much for it." The owner says, "All right, I'll sell it for that." The buyer says, "Well, I don't think it's really worth that, but I'll take the car." He gets in the car and drives it home and calls out his wife and the neighbors, "Look what a bargain I got!" That is human nature, isn't it?

> **There is gold, and a multitude of rubies: but the lips of knowledge are a precious jewel [Prov. 20:15].**

Our sense of values is all wrong today. Man is measured by material things, rather than by the knowledge he has.

> **Take his garment that is surety for a stranger: and take a pledge of him for a strange woman [Prov. 20:16].**

When you deal with certain people, you had better have them put up a little collateral. If you don't, you are sure to be taken in.

> **Bread of deceit is sweet to a man; but afterwards his mouth shall be filled with gravel [Prov. 20:17].**

A person may think he is getting by with deceit, and it may seem sweet to him. No one gets by with a thing—God will see to that.

> **He that goeth about as a talebearer revealeth secrets: therefore meddle not with him that flattereth with his lips [Prov. 20:19].**

The man who flatters you to your face and then goes off and gossips about you is the man you had better keep your eye on—even if he is a deacon in the church.

> **Whoso curseth his father or his mother, his lamp shall be put out in obscure darkness [Prov. 20:20].**

If you have a father and a mother of whom you can boast, then boast of them. If you cannot say something good about them—and a lot of folk can't—then don't say anything. That is what this proverb is saying.

This is where Ham made his mistake. Noah, his father, got drunk, and Ham exposed his father. He should have kept silence. There are certain things that you just don't run around telling everyone.

> **Man's goings are of the LORD; how can a man then understand his own way? [Prov. 20:24].**

How can a man understand his own way? We have never passed this way before—only the Spirit of God can lead us. God told Moses that he needed Him to lead him. And you and I need His leading also.

> **It is a snare to the man who devoureth that which is holy, and after vows to make inquiry [Prov. 20:25].**

Don't make a vow until you are sure of what you can do. Don't publicly dedicate your life to God until you have thought it through. God doesn't want that kind of a sentimental decision. I'm afraid there is too much of that today.

> **The spirit of man is the candle of the LORD, searching all the inward parts of the belly [Prov. 20:27].**

"The spirit of man is the candle [or lamp] of the LORD [Jehovah]." Notice it is called the candle or lamp of Jehovah, not the *light* of Jehovah. The spirit of man is only the lamp, the vessel that holds the light. Man is just a lamp, and until we are filled by the Holy Spirit, we don't become a light. Remember the parable of the ten virgins. Five of them were wise, and five were foolish. They were just lamps. Without the oil, they could not have light.

> **The glory of young men is their strength: and the beauty of old men is the grey head [Prov. 20:29].**

This proverb is saying, "Act your age." The young man is the one to be the athlete. The old man had better not try to act young. He will just make a fool of himself. He had better act his age. He should reveal a little wisdom, because that is what gray hair should indicate.

CHAPTER 21

This is one of the great chapters in the Book of Proverbs.

The king's heart is in the hand of the LORD, as the rivers of water: he turneth it whithersoever he will [Prov. 21:1].

A man may be a pharaoh in Egypt, a king of Babylon, a caesar of Rome, an Alexander the Great, a Napoleon, a Joe Stalin, an Adolph Hitler, or any great ruler of the future. Regardless of how powerful a man may become politically, it can be stated as an axiom that no man can act in independence of God. Many of these rulers thought they could, and men today may still think they can. But the truth is that no man is free from God. No man can act independently. We have a Declaration of Independence in this country. Right now it is being used to declare our independence from God. We believe in liberty; so we've declared we are free from God! However, we are not free from God. We cannot act independently. "The king's heart is in the hand of the LORD," and God is going to turn him just as He turns the course of a little babbling brook that runs down a mountainside. "As the rivers of water: he turneth it whithersoever he will." No king nor ruler nor any individual can act independently of God.

I wish we had more men in public office who express a dependence upon God and *show* it in their lives. I wish they would quit telling us that *they* have the solution for all the problems of the world. They haven't. It is a misrepresentation for any man to say that. No man is independent of Almighty God, and we need to recognize our dependence upon Him. Oh, may this country be called back to a dependence upon God before it is too late. We need a new declaration, but this time it should be a declaration of *dependence* upon Almighty God. The only way such a change can come about is by the people of this nation returning to the Word of God. That is why it is so important for us to proclaim God's Word.

Every way of a man is right in his own eyes: but the LORD pondereth the hearts [Prov. 21:2].

Here again is this matter of man's self-righteousness. Man rationalizes, but God scrutinizes. God looks at the heart. We attempt to paint up the surface so that we have the outside looking nice. We boast, "I'm a member of a church. I teach a class and serve on a committee. I'm always busy working for the church." That may all be true, but God "pondereth the hearts." The prophet Jeremiah pointed out that "The heart is deceitful above all things, and desperately wicked: who can know it?" (Jer. 17:9). Have you gone to the Lord Jesus and spoken to Him about your desperate condition? He is the Great Physician, and He is the heart specialist. He gives you a *new* heart. He was the first One who went into this business of heart transplants. He will give you a heart that can be obedient to Him.

To do justice and judgment is more acceptable to the Lord than sacrifice [Prov. 21:3].

Here we have the tremendous truth stated for us again that there is no value in simply going through a religious ritual. Remember that the Old Testament sacrifices were given because they pointed to Jesus Christ. No one was more faithful about going through those rituals than the Pharisees, the religious rulers of Jesus' day. But He denounced them in withering language. He blanched them. He scorched them. He told them they looked like beautiful monuments on the outside but inside were full of dead men's bones. Why? Because sacrifices and offerings were not pleasing to the Lord when righteousness was lacking. He said He wanted mercy, not sacrifice.

Religious ritual can suggest that you are trusting in Christ when the fact is that you are not trusting in Him. A true acceptance of the sacrifice of Jesus Christ will so transform a person that he will bring forth good works. I tell you, this gets down to the marrow and to the bone of our souls. God looks at the heart. I repeat the question I asked earlier in our study: If you were arrested for being a Christian, would there be enough evidence to convict you?

An high look, and a proud heart, and the plowing of the wicked, is sin [Prov. 21:4].

"An high look." Maybe you walked into church on Sunday morning and saw Mrs. Jones or Mr. Smith, and you just turned your head so you wouldn't have to speak to them. I was in a group recently where there was a man who had said some unlovely things about me. He acted as if he didn't see me at all—the high look. Maybe nobody noticed the high look. Maybe the person who was given the high look was unaware of it, but God saw it. God calls it a sin. In His sight it is as much a sin as to go out and get drunk. One is just as bad as the other, although we don't measure it that way. We think the one is terrible and the other doesn't matter.

"The plowing [or tillage] of the lawless is sin." This is an interesting proverb. You might see a man out plowing his field and think, *My, he is an industrious man. He certainly should be rewarded for being so industrious.* God says that when an evil man with an evil heart is doing anything—even plowing—it will not be acceptable in His sight. That means a sinner cannot give anything to God. He cannot perform a *good* work. Not only is the high look and a proud heart sinful, but what otherwise would be meritorious is *sin* in a man who is in rebellion against God. I do not think that God will bless a gift from an unsaved person. Years ago, a brewery in Dallas, Texas, gave gifts of $50,000 each to a Christian school, a denominational college, and a hospital. The school and the college returned the money. I think they did the right thing. God wouldn't use money like that.

Notice what Paul wrote to the nation of Israel: "Brethren, my heart's desire and prayer to God for Israel is, that they might be saved. For I bear them record that they have a zeal of God, but not according to knowledge. For they being ignorant of God's righteousness, and going about to establish their own righteousness, have not submitted themselves unto the righteousness of God" (Rom. 10:1–3).

When a person goes about to establish his own righteousness, God says it is *sin*. The righteousness of man is filthy rags in the sight of God.

> **The thoughts of the diligent tend only to plenteousness;**
> **but of every one that is hasty only to want.**
>
> **The getting of treasures by a lying tongue is a vanity**
> **tossed to and fro of them that seek death.**
>
> **The robbery of the wicked shall destroy them; because**
> **they refuse to do judgment [Prov. 21:5–7].**

God can use riches that are accumulated in an honest way. There is no sin in being rich. The important thing is how the money was accumulated. If the getting of riches is by lying and robbery, God will see to it that the riches will not be enjoyed. Do you get the impression that there are certain rich men today who are not really having a good time? Their riches are not what they really need.

The story is told of an Arab who was lost out in the desert. He was about to die of thirst and starvation. The poor fellow saw a package that had dropped off a caravan. He thought it might contain food or a can of beverage. He hungrily tore open the package and eagerly looked to see what it contained. He dropped it in great disappointment, and said, "It's only pearls!" Of course they were worth a fortune, but that was not his need.

My friend, God says that you can get rich, but it won't do you a bit of good unless you make money in the right way and use it for His glory.

> **The way of man is froward and strange: but as for the**
> **pure, his work is right [Prov. 21:8].**

Let me give you another translation: "The way of a guilty man is very crooked: but as for the pure, his work is right." Your life will demonstrate what kind of a person you really are. If you are right with God, that will be revealed in your life.

**It is better to dwell in a corner of the housetop, than with
a brawling woman in a wide house [Prov. 21:9].**

This is the man who did not know what true happiness was until he
got married—and then it was too late!

Down in Nashville the retired pastor of a church and I would repeatedly go down to the jail to get out a man who was a member of the
church. He would be arrested over and over again for drunkenness.
One time the retired preacher said something to me that I shall never
forget: "If I were married to the woman that he is married to, I would
drink also." Of course it is just as bad for a woman to be married to the
wrong husband. My wife and I mentioned just the other night that we
felt very sorry for a certain woman because she is married to a man
like that.

We have examples of this in the Scriptures. Job didn't do so well
with a wife. David was married to a daughter of Saul. I don't think
there was any fellowship or any real love in that marriage. She ridi-
culed David when he so joyously brought the ark to Jerusalem. She
told him he made a fool of himself, dancing before the ark. She called
his behavior disgraceful. Believe me, if you show some enthusiasm
for God, there will be a great many people who will be embarrassed. It
is tragic if it is your mate who is embarrassed.

**When the scorner is punished, the simple is made wise:
and when the wise is instructed, he receiveth knowledge [Prov. 21:11].**

We need to note these things so that we learn lessons from the experience of others around us.

**Whoso stoppeth his ears at the cry of the poor, he also
shall cry himself, but shall not be heard [Prov. 21:13].**

This is what God has said. Either it is true or it is not true. I believe it
is true, and I think we can find illustrations of this in public life in our
day.

A gift in secret pacifieth anger: and a reward in the bosom strong wrath [Prov. 21:14].

Remember that when Jacob was returning home after his years in Haran, he knew he had to face Esau for the first time after he had tricked him out of his birthright and his blessing. So he sent gifts ahead in order to pacify Esau. He didn't need to do that, because God had already taken care of Esau's attitude. But men have found that a gift in secret will pacify anger.

We can easily fall into this type of thinking: "I am going to be generous because then I'll be rewarded." Or, "I am going to forgive someone because if I do that, it will make me feel better." Jane Mershon wrote a little rhyme which illustrates this type of thinking:

> If I forgive an injury,
> Because resenting would poison me,
> I may feel noble; I may feel splendid,
> But it isn't exactly what Christ intended.

No, it isn't what Christ intended. We are to forgive because God for Christ's sake has forgiven us. That is the reason we are to be kind and tenderhearted and forgiving. Our motive for forgiving is not to make us feel better.

It is joy to the just to do judgment: but destruction shall be to the workers of iniquity.

The man that wandereth out of the way of understanding shall remain in the congregation of the dead [Prov. 21:15–16].

It is my understanding that God is saying here that you cannot rehabilitate criminals. They need to be regenerated. These fellows need the Word of God. We need to go into crime-ridden areas and preach the Word of God. We are going about things from the wrong direction according to God.

**He that loveth pleasure shall be a poor man: he that lov-
eth wine and oil shall not be rich [Prov. 21:17].**

In our contemporary society the entertainer has been glorified, and as
a result the great moral principles of life have been turned upside
down. At one time, even in the court of a king, a jester, an entertainer,
was called a fool. I don't think that has been changed in God's sight.
However, by our popular standards, the entertainers are the sacred
cows. We hear them on talk shows glorifying themselves and each
other. God still says, "He that loveth pleasure shall be a poor man: he
that loveth wine and oil shall not be rich." I can think of several entertainers who have committed suicide. One man made this statement,
"I am bored with life." Another said, "Life is not worth living." A
comedian was dying, and his friends gathered around waiting for him
to say something funny. He looked at them in stark fear and dread and
said, "This is not funny." We have things turned upside down. Television is like the wilderness of Moab. There is really nothing to see. It
becomes very boring.

**The wicked shall be a ransom for the righteous, and the
transgressor for the upright [Prov. 21:18].**

Justice demands the punishment of the guilty in order that the guilt-
less may be delivered; but, by the grace of God, Jesus Christ, the Righteous, became a ransom for the wicked. He is the "upright," and you
and I are the "transgressors."

**A wise man scaleth the city of the mighty, and casteth
down the strength of the confidence thereof [Prov.
21:22].**

He is saying that wisdom is superior to brute force. A man may be able
to build a seemingly impregnable fortress, but there will come along a
man who is smart enough to figure out how to invade it. The ancient
city of Babylon is a classic example. Belshazzar sat inside the walls of

Babylon thinking he was perfectly safe. In fact, there was an inner wall around his palace. He was certain the walls of Babylon could never be penetrated, and, of course, guards were stationed all along the walls. But the general in the camp of the enemy used his wisdom and figured a way to get into Babylon. A branch of the Euphrates River went through the city, more or less like a canal. He diverted the water back into the mainstream of the river, then he was able to march his army on the riverbed under the wall where the river had flowed. The Medo-Persian army spread into the city, and the city was taken before the Babylonians knew what was happening.

Napoleon made the statement that God is always on the side of the bigger battalions. He was wrong. He should have won at Waterloo. He was a very brilliant general, but he was not quite smart enough. He had the ability to move artillery speedily, but he got bogged down in the mud. It was old General Mud that really stopped Napoleon as he went toward Warsaw. The cavalry stumbled over the artillery that was stuck in the mud. This proverb is saying that men may depend upon riches or upon brute force, but neither will be a good enough protection.

Whoso keepeth his mouth and his tongue keepeth his soul from troubles [Prov. 21:23].

Again he mentions using the tongue aright. He has already said that if you want friends, you must show yourself friendly. So of course you are to do some talking, but you are to watch what you say. We do need friends, and the Book of Proverbs has a great deal to say about friends and enemies. Emerson put it like this:

He who has a thousand friends has not a friend to spare,
And he who has one enemy will meet him everywhere.

How true!

Proud and haughty scorner is his name, who dealeth in proud wrath [Prov. 21:24].

Have you noticed that there are two subjects which seem to appear over and over again? One is the use and abuse of the tongue. The other is pride. The uncontrolled tongue, the lying tongue, the gossiping tongue, and the proud look—God says He hates them all.

The desire of the slothful killeth him; for his hands refuse to labour [Prov. 21:25].

"Slothful" is the lazy man. There is quite a bit said about him.

He coveteth greedily all the day long: but the righteous giveth and spareth not [Prov. 21:26].

The lazy man spends his time in covetousness, and he tries to use devious devices to get money without working. There are a lot of folk who are doing that. By contrast, the righteous man is not thinking so much of getting as of giving, and God will bless him. That is the thought here.

The sacrifice of the wicked is abomination: how much more, when he bringeth it with a wicked mind? [Prov. 21:27].

The "wicked" man is the lawless man. A lawless man is one who has not bowed himself to God and come God's way. "There is a way that seemeth right unto a man" (Prov. 16:25)—that is the lawless way. He goes his way and ignores God's way. In fact, he repudiates God. This doesn't mean such a man may not be religious. He may join the church, attend regularly, sing the hymns, and put on quite a front. He may even give, but he does it with a low motive. "The sacrifice of the wicked is abomination."

A false witness shall perish: but the man that heareth speaketh constantly.

A wicked man hardeneth his face: but as for the upright, he directeth his way [Prov. 21:28–29].

There were false witnesses in the trial of the Lord Jesus. Wouldn't you hate to have been one of those false witnesses? We read in Matthew's record, "Now the chief priests, and elders, and all the council, sought false witness against Jesus, to put him to death; but found none: yea, though many false witnesses came, yet found they none. At the last came two false witnesses, and said, This fellow said, I am able to destroy the temple of God, and to build it in three days" (Matt. 26:59–61). The other false witnesses bore testimony, but it wasn't pertinent at all. These last two really lied. Jesus' response is given in the next chapter: "And Jesus stood before the governor: and the governor asked him, saying, Art thou the King of the Jews? And Jesus said unto him, Thou sayest." In other words, "You are right." "And when he was accused of the chief priests and elders, he answered nothing. Then said Pilate unto him, Hearest thou not how many things they witness against thee? And he answered him to never a word; insomuch that the governor marvelled greatly" (see Matt. 27:11–14). John's record tells us that Pilate took the Lord Jesus inside the hall of judgment and privately asked for His cooperation so he could let Him off. But he was too much of a politician to release Jesus against the wishes of the Jews. Finally, he gave in to the pressure of the mob, but all the while he knew that the witnesses against Jesus were false.

This is the trial that stands on the pages of history as being the most ignominious of all. Wouldn't you hate to have been one of those false witnesses? "A false witness shall perish."

There is no wisdom nor understanding nor counsel against the LORD [Prov. 21:30].

This is a remarkable verse of Scripture. It is so remarkable that I want to put beside it a New Testament verse that may have escaped your attention: "For we can do nothing against the truth, but for the truth" (2 Cor. 13:8).

Because I attended a liberal college and a liberal seminary, I used to become very alarmed by the inroads liberal theology was making. When I began my ministry, I thought it was my duty to sort of ring the fire bell every Sunday morning to defend the Word of God. Then this verse came to my attention. "There is no wisdom nor understanding nor counsel against the LORD." I began to realize that God is able to defend Himself, and He is able to defend His Word. "We can do nothing against the truth, but for the truth." Since I wanted to do something, I was to do it positively—accentuate the positive and leave the negative alone. I didn't need to defend the Bible; all He asked me to do was to proclaim it.

I had a letter from a man which I filed in the round file, known as the wastebasket. I didn't even read the whole letter, because he was trying to show me that the Bible is not the Word of God and used an asinine argument. I just thought, *Ho-hum, let's go on to something else because this man has a hangup of some sin in his life.* I have learned that if a man will turn to Christ, if he wants to get rid of his sin, if he does really desire to have a Savior, it will be amazing how the problems about the Bible that disturb him will be smoothed out.

The horse is prepared against the day of battle: but safety is of the LORD [Prov. 21:31].

David learned this. He wrote, "Though an host should encamp against me, my heart shall not fear: though war should rise against me, in this will I be confident" (Ps. 27:3). Asa had also learned this truth. "And Asa cried unto the LORD his God, and said, LORD, it is nothing with thee to help, whether with many, or with them that have no power: help us, O LORD our God; for we rest on thee, and in thy name we go against this multitude. O LORD, thou art our God; let not man prevail against thee" (2 Chron. 14:11). How wonderful it is to trust God.

That does not mean that we are not to be prepared. Jesus said that a strong man armed keeps his palace, and his goods are in peace. "But safety is of Jehovah." Keep your powder dry, but be sure your *faith* is in the Lord Jesus Christ and that you are resting in Him.

CHAPTER 22

Solomon, who had all that money could buy, puts material wealth in true perspective.

A good name is rather to be chosen than great riches, and loving favour rather than silver and gold [Prov. 22:1].

"Good" in most Bibles is italicized, which means that it was supplied by the translators. "A *name* is rather to be chosen"—the proverb is not speaking of the name you were called by your parents when you were born, but the name you earn by the kind of person you are.

We know that David had a group of men known as his mighty men. And they were great men. They had made a name for themselves. For example, we are told about Benaiah, "And Benaiah the son of Jehoiada, the son of a valiant man, of Kabzeel, who had done many acts, he slew two lionlike men of Moab: he went down also and slew a lion in the midst of a pit in time of snow" (2 Sam. 23:20). A lot of people won't even go to church when it snows, but this man slew a lion in the time of snow! We are told, "These things did Benaiah the son of Jehoiada, and had the name among three mighty men" (2 Sam. 23:22). He was up there in a class with the top three of the highest echelon of David's mighty men. He had a *name*. "A good name is rather to be chosen than great riches."

The rich and poor meet together: the LORD is the maker of them all [Prov. 22:2].

This means that before God all men are on the same plane. If you want to talk about a universal brotherhood of man, be very careful what you say. The Bible doesn't teach that. The Bible does teach that we are all members of the human family and that we all have a depraved nature, a nature that is alienated from God. We even need to protect ourselves from each other, because we cannot be trusted. The Bible does say that He ". . . hath made of one blood all nations of men for to dwell on all the face of the earth . . ." (Acts 17:26), and we all stand equal before Him on that basis. But we become the sons of God—not just because we are human beings—but by faith in Jesus Christ. The Lord Jesus said to the religious rulers of His day, "Ye are of your father the devil . . ." (John 8:44). So actually there are two families in the world: children of God and children of the devil. Obviously, the universal fatherhood of God does not exist.

Now notice that the proverb says: "The Lord is the maker of them all." We are all His by *creation*. God is the Creator of all but not the Father of all.

A prudent man foreseeth the evil, and hideth himself: but the simple pass on, and are punished [Prov. 22:3].

Do you want to be a smart man? Then make arrangements for the future. There are many men today who will help you make arrangements for the future. There are all kinds of insurance companies and agencies. There are people willing to make arrangements for your old age, for the care of your children, and all that sort of thing. But I'm thinking of the next step. What about that? What about your eternal future? The Scripture calls a man a fool who has not made preparation for eternity.

When I was a young man in Nashville, Tennessee, I was very far from the Lord for awhile. I remember a fine young couple, who belonged to rich families. At a dance one night they announced their engagement, and then later they were married. Of course they made the society page of the newspaper. They had bought a very lovely southern home with those white columns out in front. They had searched everywhere for antiques, and they furnished that home beautifully. On their wedding trip they went to the Great Smokies in East Tennessee and North Carolina. Going up into the mountains, they went around a curve and were hit and knocked off the highway down a precipice. The car caught fire, and they were both killed. The parents of the couple simply locked the door to their lovely home and left it unoccupied.

For years after I was saved, I would go by that house and reflect on all the preparation they had put into that house; yet they had not lived in it for one hour. And they went into eternity totally unprepared. Oh, how important it is for us to be making preparation for eternity!

Train up a child in the way he should go: and when he is old, he will not depart from it [Prov. 22:6].

We are to train up a child concerning the way he should go. What he is saying is that God has a way He wants him to go, and parents are to find out that way. They are not to bring up a child in the way *they* think he should go, but in the way *God* wants him to go.

The slothful man saith, There is a lion without, I shall be slain in the streets [Prov. 22:13].

Here we have the lazy man again. This verse has its humor in it, too. Believe me, the lazy man is full of excuses. It's too cold outside so he cannot go out to plow. Here is his new excuse: "There is a lion without, I shall be slain in the streets." I think he was lyin' about the lion!

Foolishness is bound in the heart of a child; but the rod of correction shall drive it far from him [Prov. 22:15].

These instructions for child rearing are repeated for emphasis. Children need discipline. Proper discipline will not provoke the child to anger. Neither will it be simply the venting of our own anger. Proper discipline will help the child overcome his foolishness.

Remove not the ancient landmark, which thy fathers have set [Prov. 22:28].

When God brought the children of Israel from Egypt, He gave them a land. Sometimes we forget that He also gave to each tribe a particular section of that land. And He gave to each family in each tribe a particular parcel of that land. Each family was to put up boundary markers for their own parcel of land. These boundary markers were generally piles of stones.

Down in front of my house in the sidewalk there is a little brass circle at one end of my lot and another little brass circle at the other end of my lot, marking where my lot begins and where it ends. This whole area used to be an avocado grove, and I have a notion that the markers were put in when it was converted into a subdivision. It was done to make sure that I stay within my own lot.

God gave Israel definite rules regarding their markers: "Thou shalt not remove thy neighbour's landmark, which they of old time have set in thine inheritance, which thou shalt inherit in the land that the LORD thy God giveth thee to possess it" (Deut. 19:14). These markers went from generation to generation and were very important. When a man got old and feeble and his eyesight began to fail him, his neighbor might want to slip over and move the marker a couple of feet to increase his own parcel of land. God said that kind of thing was forbidden. It would be totally dishonest, of course.

Now I am going to make a spiritual application of this. You may think I am square when I say this, but I believe that today we have seen the landmarks of the Christian faith removed. They have been removed by what was first called modernism, and now is called liberalism. These folk with a liberal viewpoint say, "This old landmark, this doctrine that was taught in the days of the apostle Paul, is no longer relevant. We have learned so much that we don't need the doctrine of the plenary inspiration of the Scriptures. We can do away with that. And we can do away with the doctrine of the deity of Christ." These distinguishing doctrines of the Christian faith have been pretty well washed out by a great many of the old line denominations on the basis that we must come up to date. Now I want to say this: Instead of moving forward and removing landmarks, we need to start moving backward to get back to many of the ancient landmarks.

Those ancient landmarks made this nation great. The landmarks of moral values, the spiritual truths, the biblical basis—all have been removed. We look around us today and hear everyone telling what he thinks the solution is, and it is always a sociological or psychological solution. I haven't heard any of our leaders suggesting a biblical solution. I say that we need to get back to the good old landmarks which our nation had at the beginning.

This chapter concludes with a word of commendation for the man who is diligent.

> **Seest thou a man diligent in his business? he shall stand before kings; he shall not stand before mean men [Prov. 22:29].**

God says that He intends to reward the diligent man. You remember that the Lord Jesus said that in eternity His commendation would be: ". . . Well done, thou good and faithful servant . . ." (Matt. 25:21). His commendation will not be based on the amount of work you have done, or on the number of people to whom you have witnessed, or how hard you have worked, but on how faithful you have been to the task He has given you. He may have given you the task of being a mother to a little one in the home. Moses' mother was faithful in that way, and her name is recorded in the Word of God. The reward will be for faithfulness.

The apostle Paul put it like this in Romans 12:10–11 (and I'll give you a little more meaningful translation of my own): "As to brotherly love, have family affection one to another; for your code of honor, deferring to one another. Never flag in zeal, be aglow (fervent) with the Spirit, serving the Lord." It all adds up to being faithful to God—and that is what we should be.

CHAPTER 23

Our young man has been attending the school of wisdom for quite some time now. I think we will have a graduation ceremony soon.

> **When thou sittest to eat with a ruler, consider diligently what is before thee:**
>
> **And put a knife to thy throat, if thou be a man given to appetite.**
>
> **Be not desirous of his dainties: for they are deceitful meat [Prov. 23:1–3].**

I can state this in very commonplace language: Don't make a pig of yourself when you are invited out to eat—especially if you are invited to a place that serves you gourmet food, the type of food that you are not accustomed to eating. In fact, it would be better, he says, to cut your throat than make a pig of yourself! In other words, be temperate in all things. Use moderation and self-control, even when you eat.

In our day the theory is that some folk eat, not because of real hunger, but because of a psychological factor. Some people eat when they are under tension, when they are uptight. We should be relaxed and enjoy our meals but eat in moderation.

> **Labour not to be rich: cease from thine own wisdom.**
>
> **Wilt thou set thine eyes upon that which is not? for riches certainly make themselves wings; they fly away as an eagle toward heaven [Prov. 23:4–5].**

You have probably noticed that the United States dollar has an eagle on it. Believe me, that eagle will fly away if you're not careful with it. I find that the eagles on my dollars take off all the time. We cannot depend on riches.

The whole thought here is this: There is nothing wrong in being rich. There is nothing wrong in working to be rich. However, don't make that the goal in life. Wealth should not be the very object of our hearts. Some men have a lust, a thirst, a covetousness to make the almighty dollar, and the dollar becomes their god. A child of God is not to do that.

A wealthy man told me, "I do not make money for the sake of money. I make money for what it can do. At first I made money for what it could do for *me*. Now I make money for what it can do for *God*." There is nothing wrong in a man becoming wealthy. The wrong comes when there is the overweening desire of the heart for money. That is covetousness; actually it is modern idolatry.

In the United States we do not find people bowing down to worship idols. However, we do find people busily engaging their whole lives in the worship of the almighty dollar. When I pastored a church in the downtown financial district of Los Angeles, I found that men, even including some Christian men, were far more zealous in coming down early on a Monday morning to watch the stock market open than they were on Sunday morning to attend church service. I met such a man rushing to the stock market display at the brokerage on a Monday morning. He met me, greeted me cordially, and told me what he was going to do. I mentioned to him that we had been missing him at church. He said, "Well, you know, I haven't been feeling very well." That is interesting. He didn't feel well enough to come to church, but he was well enough to worship his god very early on a Monday morning. That's covetousness, and that is what the proverb is talking about. That is a false god, and that false god is an eagle that will fly away at any moment.

Eat thou not the bread of him that hath an evil eye, neither desire thou his dainty meats:

For as he thinketh in his heart, so is he: Eat and drink, saith he to thee; but his heart is not with thee.

The morsel which thou hast eaten shalt thou vomit up, and lose thy sweet words [Prov. 23:6–8].

Here is good advice for the young man, especially for the young preacher. On several occasions I have been warned by ministers with whom I have had Bible conferences. They have said something like this: "Now you will be invited to dinner by so-an-so, but you be very careful what you say if you go there because they are name-droppers, as you will find out. They will ask you certain questions, and they will use your answers against you later on." Well, when I am relaxed at a meal and talking with friends, I can easily say something that can be misconstrued.

Not too long ago I had such an experience. A couple used certain things that I had said about a personal friend of mine. I was just kidding, because I love that man. He is my brother in the Lord, and we play golf together. He said to me, "What in the world are you saying about me?" I told him, and he laughed. He said, "Those people took what you said and gave it a twist." But he said that he had been over to see them and had said something about me that would be coming back to me. And it did! He kids me too, and they had twisted what he had said about me. These were the kind of folk that Solomon had in mind when he wrote, "Eat thou not the bread of him that hath an evil eye." When you are invited out to dinner, make sure that you know the people with whom you are to dine. They may not be as cordial as you think they are.

Remove not the old landmark; and enter not into the fields of the fatherless [Prov. 23:10].

Now we have this remark about the old landmark again. If you have lost your faith—well, you'd better not pass that on to your children, because they will really pay for it. You probably had a good background and Christian parents, but your children will have no background to protect them.

Dr. J. Gresham Machen once said, "America is coasti
on a godly ancestry." I agree with him, and it was my ge
had the godly ancestry; but we did not pass it on to o1
was my generation that produced the younger generation u...
blaming for everything.

> **Withhold not correction from the child: for if thou
> beatest him with the rod, he shall not die [Prov. 23:13].**

Now we have been over this before. Remember that Paul adds to this
that the parent is not to correct the child in a fit of anger. The correction is to be for discipline, not punishment. If the discipline doesn't
help to develop the character of that child, it is no good.

We should not tell our children that we are punishing them. It
would be better to tell them that we are disciplining them. Paul tells
the fathers not to provoke the children to wrath, but ". . . bring them
up in the instruction and discipline of the Lord" (Eph. 6:4). We need
to remember that it is the discipline and the instruction *of the Lord.*
That is important.

> **Hear thou, my son, and be wise, and guide thine heart
> in the way.**

> **Be not among winebibbers; among riotous eaters of
> flesh:**

> **For the drunkard and the glutton shall come to poverty:
> and drowsiness shall clothe a man with rags [Prov.
> 23:19–21].**

Be very careful of the company you keep, young man. Birds of a
feather flock together. Evil companions produce evil manners. This is
a special warning to the young people.

> **Hearken unto thy father that begat thee, and despise not
> thy mother when she is old [Prov. 23:22].**

he young man is almost ready to graduate from the school of wisdom. His parents may be getting old. His dad may be a square, he may even be a bit senile, but the old folks still have a lot more sense than the young man has.

You would hear an example of this if you could only talk to Absalom. He would tell you that his dad had more sense than he had. He thought he could win a rebellion against his father, King David, but old David was a warhorse. When that boy moved out to the battlefield, he made a mistake. He should never have left Jerusalem because David knew his way around on the battlefield, and it was fatal for that boy.

Buy the truth, and sell it not; also wisdom, and instruction, and understanding [Prov. 23:23].

You and I do not need to buy truth with money. It is available to us without money and without price. "Ho, every one that thirsteth, come ye to the waters, and he that hath no money; come ye, buy, and eat; yea, come, buy wine and milk without money and without price" (Isa. 55:1). Christ is all of this for the child of God. He is truth and wisdom and understanding. The brilliant young Pharisee, Saul, who became the apostle Paul, tells us about it: "But of him are ye in Christ Jesus, who of God is made unto us wisdom, and righteousness, and sanctification, and redemption" (1 Cor. 1:30).

My son, give me thine heart, and let thine eyes observe my ways [Prov. 23:26].

Someone may say, "Dr. McGee, I thought you said that God doesn't want our old dirty, filthy hearts." That's right. He can't use them. But when He says, "My son, give me thine heart," He is not talking to the unsaved man; He is talking to His son. He is talking to the one to whom He has given a new heart, a new nature, who has been born again. Now He says to that one, "I want you to come to Me and I want you to yield yourself to Me. If you love Me, keep My commandments." If you have been redeemed by the blood of Christ, you can sing:

Take my poor heart, and let it be
Forever closed to all but Thee.
Take my love, my Lord; I pour
At Thy feet its treasure-store.

For a whore is a deep ditch; and a strange woman is a narrow pit [Prov. 23:27].

If anyone thought I was wrong in saying the stranger was a harlot, then here is a parallelism that shows the two are synonymous. That should answer that question.

She also lieth in wait as for a prey, and increaseth the transgressors among men [Prov. 23:28].

The lives of two men illustrate this. There is the story of Judah in the Book of Genesis. That is a sorry chapter which tells his story when he went in to a harlot. Then there is the story of Samson. If he were here today, he would say, "I found out that a harlot is treacherous—she can betray you without a qualm."

Who hath woe? who hath sorrow? who hath contentions? who hath babbling? who hath wounds without cause? who hath redness of eyes?

They that tarry long at the wine; they that go to seek mixed wine [Prov. 23:29–30].

Here again is a warning against this matter of drunkenness. We have heard many warnings about wine and women—but there is no song. Because—

At the last it biteth like a serpent, and stingeth like an adder.

Thine eyes shall behold strange women, and thine heart shall utter perverse things.

Yea, thou shalt be as he that lieth down in the midst of the sea, or as he that lieth upon the top of a mast.

They have stricken me, shalt thou say, and I was not sick; they have beaten me, and I felt it not: when shall I awake? I will seek it yet again [Prov. 23:32–35].

What a picture of drunkenness this is!

CHAPTER 24

This is the last chapter of the proverbs of Solomon which he wrote and arranged. After this we come to proverbs of Solomon that were arranged by the men of Hezekiah. Evidently Solomon wrote a great many proverbs. We have only a very small percentage of the total number. These are tremendous truths that have ben placed in a very small compass. They can grip and direct our lives.

> **Be not thou envious against evil men, neither desire to be with them.**
>
> **For their heart studieth destruction, and their lips talk of mischief [Prov. 24:1–2].**

This has been presented to us before. We find a repetition of the things which are important. For example, a great deal has been said about the use of the tongue and about pride and about being a fool. They are things that are constantly emphasized, because they are translated into life. We find these folk, not only on the sidewalks of New York, but in your town and my town. That is the reason I said you will find a proverb to fit every person you know. We have already found a great number which fit different characters in the Bible.

Psalm 73, a psalm of Asaph, deals with the same subject as our verse here in Proverbs. Asaph writes, "For I was envious at the foolish, when I saw the prosperity of the wicked. . . . They are not in trouble as other men; neither are they plagued like other men . . . . They set their mouth against the heavens, and their tongue walketh through the earth" (Ps. 73:3–9). Asaph was disturbed about that. I am of the opinion that you have been disturbed by it also. I certainly have had these feelings. I remember as a poor boy that I couldn't understand why I had to be poor and drop out of school to work when I was only fourteen years of age. I looked about me and saw other boys who were well able to go to school but were dropping out because they hated it. I had a real question about it, because I had such a desire for an education.

Now Solomon deals with this matter: "Be not thou envious against evil men, neither desire to be with them." Why? A day of reckoning is coming. Asaph said he didn't understand why the wicked prospered—"Until I went into the sanctuary of God; then understood I their end" (Ps. 73:17, italics mine). God will deal with them.

As we look out upon the world, we see a great deal of injustice, and there is very little that you and I can do about it. We have been in a generation that has protested about everything. They have attempted to equalize a great many things in this world. I don't think all of the protesting has solved any problem because the problem is in the *heart* of man. It is the *heart* of man that must be changed. God is the One who is going to level this thing off someday. We can trust Him to do that.

You and I need to recognize our place in life. It is going to make us happier people if we realize that God has put each of us in our own particular place to fulfill a purpose here on earth. I look at wicked men who are prosperous, and I don't understand it. I have told God a dozen times that I don't understand it. Don't you be afraid to tell it to God just as Asaph did. The important thing is for you to go on with God, trusting Him to work it all out.

We need to learn to look at things from God's point of view. The Bible is full of instances of wicked men who came to a bad end. It starts with Cain in the Book of Genesis. Even a man like Lot, although he was a saved man, chose to live in the city of Sodom and prospered there, but there came a day when he wished he had not moved to Sodom. It was a sad mistake for him to do that. So if you will go through the Word of God, you will find people who prospered for a time and then see how judgment has come time and time again. This is very important for us to understand.

Through wisdom is an house builded; and by understanding it is established:

And by knowledge shall the chambers be filled with all precious and pleasant riches [Prov. 24:3–4].

This is a wonderful picture of what we are to do. A man builds a house, and then he fills that house with furniture, with lovely pictures and tapestries, with beautiful personal items and valuable things. It is a pleasure to see a home like that, a beautiful home that is tastefully furnished.

You and I ought to be building us a house down here, a house of wisdom, a house of knowledge. We should begin to store our minds and our hearts with all kinds of wonderful furniture, vases, pictures and lovely things. This was the thing that Paul admonished Timothy: "Study to shew thyself approved unto God, a workman that needeth not to be ashamed, rightly dividing the word of truth" (2 Tim. 2:15). And you and I should be filling our hearts and lives with the Word of God. Oh, my friend, let's be working toward a beautiful mansion; let's not be satisfied with a hovel.

When I was down in South America visiting with a missionary, he took me to some of the homes in his area. Many of them were what we would call a "lean-to" made out of old boards. Many of them were decaying, dilapidated places. Inside there was no place to sit, not even a chair. There would be a blanket or a sheepskin in a corner where the family would sleep; there was no bed. The cooking was done on the outside. I thought how tragic it was. Frankly, it made me sick just thinking of the poverty of those people down in South America. But, my friend, up here in North America I know many Christians who should have spent their lives building a lovely home—a spiritual home—and filling it with all kinds of wonderful treasures out of the Word of God. Instead, all they have is a little hovel. And when I look inside—oh, the ignorance! There is nothing there; it is absolutely bare.

In talking to a group of preachers just the other day, they agreed with me on this: the greatest tragedy in our churches today is the ignorance of the church members. Oh, the poor little empty houses they have! "Through wisdom is an house builded; and by understanding it is established: and by knowledge shall the chambers be filled with all precious and pleasant riches."

> **A wise man is strong; yea, a man of knowledge increaseth strength.**
>
> **For by wise counsel thou shalt make thy war: and in multitude of counsellors there is safety [Prov. 24:5-6].**

There are many resources for us to use today. Not only do we have people to whom we can turn for counsel, but we also have the Word of God. I don't believe in this method of opening the Bible to look at some verse at the time of making a decision. That is not good. The Word of God is not a roulette wheel for us to turn and hope it stops at the right place. We need to know what the whole Bible says. We need to read Moses and Joshua and Samuel and David and Micah and Zechariah and Matthew and Paul and John. They are all our counselors. We can appeal to all of them at any time of decision.

> **If thou faint in the day of adversity, thy strength is small [Prov. 24:10].**

He is saying something here that is rather important: It takes a *man* to do a man's *job*. We use the old bromide, "Never send a boy to do a man's work." God uses these times of real stress and strain and testing to develop our spiritual character. That is the way He enables us to grow. It is in the hour of trial that you and I manifest the spiritual strength that we have.

It is a great comfort for us to know that many of God's men turned and ran when their test came. Elijah had been so brave on the top of Mount Carmel, but when he heard that Jezebel was after him with the intention of killing him, he took off and ran for the wilderness until he got down to Beer-sheba. He left his servant there and continued on in the desert, climbed under a juniper tree, and said, ". . . LORD, let me die" (cf. 1 Kings 19:4).

When David was hunted by King Saul, he didn't have a moment of peace. David said that he was hunted like a partridge in the mountains and that one of these days they would catch him and put him to death. He became very discouraged. But both David and Elijah learned in that hour that the Lord would and did strengthen them.

If thou forbear to deliver them that are drawn unto death, and those that are ready to be slain;

If thou sayest, Behold, we knew it not; doth not he that pondereth the heart consider it? and he that keepeth thy soul, doth not he know it? and shall not he render to every man according to his works? [Prov. 24:11–12].

Now there is somebody you could help, and you *know* you could. There is somebody to whom you could witness for Christ, and you may be the only one to whom he would listen.

Recently I talked with a man who feels that he has been responsible for the suicide of a loved one. He says that he knew he should have done something. I'm of the opinion that he should have, but he didn't do it. A man can be under great conviction because he neglected to do something at a time when he should have done it.

The Lord God is the One who ponders the heart. In such an instance when we know we have failed to do something that we should have done, there is nothing left but to turn to the Lord and say, "Lord, forgive me. I failed. I come to You now asking You to strengthen me and help me." The Lord will hear that kind of prayer. He will deliver a man from being overwhelmed by the grief and guilt of his failure.

We do well to mark the importance of this proverb and reach out to people who are in need of our help.

For a just man falleth seven times, and riseth up again: but the wicked shall fall into mischief [Prov. 24:16].

"A just man falleth seven times, and riseth up again." Seven is the number of completeness. It means man just keeps on falling. But the just man will get up again. Do you know a man like that? Simon Peter was one. But then notice that "the wicked shall fall into mischief." That is Judas. This proverb perfectly illustrates those two disciples of our Lord. Peter was a man who was constantly falling. We may say that he failed when he tried to walk on the water. I don't really think that he failed, because he *did* walk on the water. He walked on the water to come to Jesus, but when he took his eyes off Jesus and looked at those rolling waves, he began to go under; he began to sink. But remember that the Lord rescued him and he walked back to the boat with Jesus. But Peter certainly fell the night the Lord Jesus was arrested. He denied his Lord three times. Again and again and again Peter failed the Lord. But he always got up and went on with the Lord.

A man came to me when I was a pastor in Pasadena. He said, "I have failed so many times and I am ashamed to go back to the Lord and tell Him again that I have failed and want to start over." I told him, "You may be ashamed, but the Lord is not. He is ready to start you out again." Then he asked, "How many times do you suppose you can fail and still come back?" I told him, "I don't know, but I am working up in the hundreds myself, and I still go to Him." It is so important for us to understand that we can go back to our Heavenly Father and tell Him that we stumbled and got dirty again. He will put us right back into His service. How wonderful it is to have a Heavenly Father like that!

> **Rejoice not when thine enemy falleth, and let not thine heart be glad when he stumbleth [Prov. 24:17].**

When you hear that something bad has happened to someone you haven't really liked very much, don't you say, "I'm glad that happened to him"? Now, don't tell me you have never said that, because human nature is like that. If you haven't said it, you've *thought* it. God says, "Rejoice not when thine enemy falleth." That is not the way to solve the problem. Why?

> **Lest the LORD see it, and it displease him, and he turn away his wrath from him [Prov. 24:18].**

If you rejoice when your enemy falls, the Lord may turn around and start prospering that man. Then you really will be miserable. So there is a very practical reason for not rejoicing when your enemy falls.

Fret not thyself because of evil men, neither be thou envious at the wicked [Prov. 24:19].

You may think, *We have just read that.* Yes, it is the same thought as verse 1 of this chapter. Then why is it repeated? Again, it is to show us how important this is. The Lord wants us to learn this.

Have you noticed that some of the parables and certain of the miracles of our Lord are repeated? For example, the feeding of the five thousand is recorded in all four Gospels. Each of the Gospel writers adds details which are peculiar to his Gospel. The miracle was of such importance that it is recorded for us four times. And the teaching of this proverb needs to be repeated because of its importance.

From verse 23 to the end of the chapter there is sort of an appendix which is introduced by, "These things also belong to the wise."

These things also belong to the wise. It is not good to have respect of persons in judgment [Prov. 24:23].

Here is something else the young man should learn before he graduates: "It is not good to have respect of persons in judgment"—that is, it is not good to show partiality in judgment. This is an important matter in daily living and something which is needed today. Men in public office need to know this. Employers need to know this. Anyone in any position of authority needs to know this. There should not be a system of favorites, but justice should be equal to all.

He that saith unto the wicked, Thou art righteous; him shall the people curse, nations shall abhor him [Prov. 24:24].

There is a great deal of that today. Wicked men are *commended*. Often the wicked man is called a righteous man. That is one of the worst things that could take place.

> **Say not, I will do so to him as he hath done to me: I will render to the man according to his work [Prov. 24:29].**

This repeats what we have been hearing over and over again. It is the same message which Paul wrote to the Romans: ". . . Vengeance is mine; I will repay, saith the Lord" (Rom. 12:19).

> **Yet a little sleep, a little slumber, a little folding of the hands to sleep:**
>
> **So shall thy poverty come as one that travelleth; and thy want as an armed man [Prov. 24:33–34].**

This young man is going to graduate from college. He may know a lot and he may have other good qualities, but if he is lazy, he will find *that* to be the greatest handicap he could have in life.

CHAPTER 25

This is a new division of the Book of Proverbs. These are still proverbs of Solomon, but they were put together by the men of Hezekiah. The Septuagint calls them "the friends of Hezekiah."

> **These are also proverbs of Solomon, which the men of Hezekiah king of Judah copied out.**

> **It is the glory of God to conceal a thing: but the honour of kings is to search out a matter [Prov. 25:1–2].**

This is the way the proverb states what the Lord Jesus said: "Search the scriptures . . ." (John 5:39). Paul wrote the same thing: "Study to shew thyself approved unto God, a workman that needeth not to be ashamed, rightly dividing the word of truth" (2 Tim. 2:15).

We are to "search out a matter." Even then we need to recognize that there are a great many things that God has not revealed to us at all. I doubt if we would be able to understand them if He did. They are inscrutable; they are beyond the comprehension of man. As He made it very clear: "For as the heavens are higher than the earth, so are my ways higher than your ways, and my thoughts than your thoughts" (Isa. 55:9).

However, what God has revealed to us, we should study; we should consider it. It is important that we recognize our need to search the Word of God and to study it.

> **The heaven for height, and the earth for depth, and the heart of kings is unsearchable [Prov. 25:3].**

Sometimes we don't understand what our rulers are doing. They probably have justification for it, because they know things that we do not know. Neither can we understand God's ways, but we are never to sit in judgment upon what God does because whatever God does is *right*—it is the proper thing to do.

> **Take away the dross from the silver, and there shall come forth a vessel for the finer.**
>
> **Take away the wicked from before the king, and his throne shall be established in righteousness [Prov. 25:4–5].**

I think one of the worst things that can happen to any individual is to have an evil adviser, someone who leads you into difficulty and trouble and sin. I thank God for a man in my life who led me away from that, because there was another man who had led me in the wrong direction. Think how important this is to the man in high position. A man who makes a decision in business that would affect a great many employees or a man in government whose decision would affect a great segment of the population needs to have the right kind of advisers around.

> **Put not forth thyself in the presence of the king, and stand not in the place of great men:**
>
> **For better it is that it be said unto thee, Come up hither; than that thou shouldest be put lower in the presence of the prince whom thine eyes have seen [Prov. 25:6–7].**

"Put not forth" could be translated "display not." You will remember that the Lord Jesus gave a parable to illustrate this great truth, and He did it because the religious rulers of His day were paying no attention to this proverb at all. When a great and important man invited many of his friends for dinner, he had reserved places at the table for certain ones he wanted to honor. But when the dinner bell was rung, there was a mad rush to get the best places at the table. They almost turned the thing over, I imagine, as they rushed in to get the most prominent places. The Lord Jesus was present there that day and apparently waited until everyone else had gone in. Then He said something to correct them: "When you're invited to a dinner, don't try to get the best place. You should purposely take the lowest place. Then when the one who has invited you comes in and sees you taking the lowest place—if you are his honored guest—he may say to you, 'Come on up here.' Now, if someone else has taken that place, the host would have to tap him on the shoulder and say, 'You go down and take the lowest place'" (cf. Luke 14:7–10).

There are people whom we call "pushy" today—they are pushing themselves. We have people who are pushy in Christian circles. They are ambitious. They want to get ahead in Christian things. That is a tragedy. Maybe you can't blame a man in the business world for trying to get ahead, but in Christian work it ought not to be.

Go not forth hastily to strive, lest thou know not what to do in the end thereof, when thy neighbour hath put thee to shame [Prov. 25:8].

Now, again, the Lord Jesus gave a parable about this. He said in essence, "When a king is ready to go forth to war, he ought to sit down and see whether he's going to be able to get the victory. And if he sees that he can't carry on the warfare, then he ought to send an ambassador to make a peace treaty with the enemy" (cf. Luke 14:31–32).

We have an example of this in the Old Testament in King Josiah. He was a good king, and he led the last great revival that Judah had. There was a great turning back to God under his leadership, but he made one grave mistake. Somehow just one flaw sometimes spoils the life of an otherwise great man. Josiah was a great man and an outstanding man of God, but he made this bad mistake. Pharaoh Nechoh, king of Egypt, came to make war, not against Josiah at all, but against an altogether different enemy. But when Josiah came out against him, Pharaoh Nechoh told Josiah, "Now look, I didn't come up to fight you." But Josiah (he was a young man) had gone out to fight. I guess he thought it was the Lord's will. (A great many of us blame the Lord for the mistakes in our decisions.) Josiah got into real trouble and lost the battle. In fact, he was killed in the battle there at Megiddo where the war of Armageddon will be fought. Josiah made a big mistake by meddling when he should not have done that at all. That is the thing the Lord wants us to see in this proverb (cf. 2 Kings 23:28–30).

> **Debate thy cause with thy neighbour himself; and discover not a secret to another:**
>
> **Lest he that heareth it put thee to shame, and thine infamy turn not away [Prov. 25:9–10].**

You could cause a great deal of trouble by criticizing your neighbor to the man down the street. If your neighbor has faults, go and talk to him personally.

> **A word fitly spoken is like apples of gold in pictures of silver [Prov. 25:11].**

Isn't that a lovely one? That is just a beautiful simile. "Apples of gold"—we do have a Golden Delicious apple today, but apparently the fruit referred to here is the orange. Oranges, as well as other citrus fruits, were common and native to Israel. Today they grow some of the finest oranges in the world. An orange is a beautiful fruit. Someone will think I am promoting oranges because I live in California, but oranges were plentiful in Palestine at the time of Solomon.

As we go through the Word of God, we find that certain individuals said in a wonderful way just the right word at the right time. Sometimes it's a good word. Sometimes it's a word of rebuke. But the words were necessary, and they were "fitly spoken." The words fit into the picture. They were the proper thing to say.

This is something that most of us ought to pray about: what we should say and at what time. We need to recognize that many times we say the wrong thing at the right time, or sometimes we have the knack of saying the right thing but at the wrong time. And there are times when we probably ought not to open our mouths at all.

I'm sure we all know some dear Christian who has a reputation of being able to say just the right thing at the right time—"a word fitly spoken." There was a dear saint of God who lived in the country in middle Tennessee years ago. She had a reputation for always saying something very nice to the preacher at the end of every morning service. Very frankly, people would linger to hear what she had to say, because there were times they couldn't think of anything good to say about the sermon that they had heard. And one time they had a visiting preacher who was just a little worse than any they had ever had before. I tell you, people were interested that morning. What in the world could she say *nice* to that preacher about the sermon he had preached? So when she went out, she said to him, "Pastor, I want you to know that I did enjoy your sermon, because this morning you had one of the most wonderful texts in Scripture." Now that is "a word fitly spoken." It was like oranges in a picture frame of silver. The golden orange and the silver frame blend very well, as you know.

As an earring of gold, and an ornament of fine gold, so is a wise reprover upon an obedient ear [Prov. 25:12].

You have seen a woman's beautiful earring. In our day some men are wearing earrings, although I never saw one that I thought was attractive; but you have seen a woman beautifully wearing an earring. That describes the effect of a wise reprover upon an obedient ear. There are times when a person should be reproved and rebuked. We are living in a day when if we rebuke someone, especially if it is done publicly, people will say, "My, you certainly have lost that individual. You'll never be able to win him." Friend, if he's the right kind of individual, you'll win him. And if he's the wrong kind, you wouldn't be able to win him anyway. There are times that a reproof should be made.

As the cold of snow in the time of harvest, so is a faithful messenger to them that send him: for he refresheth the soul of his masters [Prov. 25:13].

In that land it gets really hot at the time of harvest. And in that day they would go up to Mount Hermon and pack some of the snow and bring it down. I tell you, the snow was *good*. How wonderful it tasted!

That is what a faithful messenger is. No wonder the Lord is going to say to some, ". . . Well done, thou good and faithful servant" (Matt. 25:21).

We all like to have around us *faithful* people. A man wants a faithful wife. He appreciates faithful children. An employer wants faithful employees. A pastor wants a faithful staff and a faithful congregation. And the people want a faithful pastor. Faithfulness is a wonderful quality. It is like a good, cold drink on a very hot day to have someone with us who is faithful.

> **Whoso boasteth himself of a false gift is like clouds and wind without rain [Prov. 25:14].**

Some men boast of gifts they don't have. When I was a pastor, I would get letters from men who would tell me how wonderful they were. I remember one man wrote me, and he said he was an evangelist, a Bible teacher, a singer, and a pianist. He could do everything, and he wanted to hold a meeting at our church. I read the letter to the officers of the church, and they began to laugh. They said to me, "Why don't you invite him?" I said, "I'd never invite that man for two reasons. The first reason is, if he's the kind of man he says he is, after our people had heard him, they'd never want to hear me again! The second reason is I have a notion that he is a man who is boasting of a gift he does not have." What a picture this is!

And this is the picture of the apostates in the last days. Jude describes them in the most vivid language. He speaks of them as being clouds without water, fruit trees without fruit, "Raging waves of the sea, foaming out their own shame . . ." (Jude 12-13).

> **Hast thou found honey? eat so much as is sufficient for thee, lest thou be filled therewith, and vomit it [Prov. 25:16].**

In the Old Testament, honey illustrates *natural* sweetness. There was no honey permitted in the bread or meal offering, because that offering speaks of Jesus Christ in His humanity. There was no natural sweetness in Him.

Have you ever met someone who was so sweet, who said so many sweet things it almost made you sick? Notice what it says here. Don't take in too much honey because it will make you sick at your tummy.

> **Withdraw thy foot from thy neighbour's house; lest he be weary of thee, and so hate thee [Prov. 25:17].**

Oh, this is a good one! Don't spend too much time at the neighbor's, or else you may overhear a conversation in the kitchen where the lady of the house says, "I wish that old gossip would go home and stay home." It's better not to wear out your welcome at a place. That is what he is saying here.

> **Confidence in an unfaithful man in time of trouble is like a broken tooth, and a foot out of joint [Prov. 25:19].**

For example, Judas was a bad toothache, and he was foot trouble—he was both of them. You have probably met someone like that in your life.

> **If thine enemy be hungry, give him bread to eat; and if he be thirsty, give him water to drink:**
>
> **For thou shalt heap coals of fire upon his head, and the Lord shall reward thee [Prov. 25:21–22].**

We find that the Lord Jesus repeats this principle, and Paul does too. It is very important.

> **The north wind driveth away rain: so doth an angry countenance a backbiting tongue [Prov. 25:23].**

We are living in a day of sweetness and light when we are not supposed to rebuke anyone for anything. Every now and then I get a letter from some lovely saint who rebukes me for being hard on certain groups and certain movements. May I say that I believe that is what I should do. "The north wind driveth away rain." An angry countenance will take care of a backbiting tongue; it will take care of those who are teaching falsely today. I think they should be dealt with, and I intend to continue to speak out when it is important to speak out.

It would be wonderful if we could have sweetness and light all the time, but we are living in a world in which there are serpents along the pathway of life. There are pitfalls in our path: there is false doctrine and false teaching of the Word of God. And I want to speak out, but I hope I do it in a spirit of love. I have no intention of hurting any individual, but I do try to give out the truth of God. I find ample justification for that in the Word of God and here is one verse for it.

It is better to dwell in the corner of the housetop, than with a brawling woman and in a wide house [Prov. 25:24].

We have had this pointed out to us several times already. Solomon, who had so many wives, must have had a lot of trouble with some of them. Maybe that is why he mentioned this so often. I have wondered if he had some backseat drivers when he would go for a ride in his chariot.

As cold waters to a thirsty soul, so is good news from a far country [Prov. 25:25].

Have you heard from home lately? Or have you written home to mother? That is important. But there is something far greater in this verse than first meets the eye.

There has come good news from a far country. The Lord Jesus said, "I came forth from the Father, and am come into the world: again, I leave the world, and go to the Father" (John 16:28). In that brief period of time, as John Wesley said, God was contracted to a span, and He wrought out your salvation and mine. That is the good news that has come to us from a far country. By the way, have you received Him? Have you accepted Him? He is the Water of Life. He is "cold waters to a thirsty soul."

> **A righteous man falling down before the wicked is as a troubled fountain, and a corrupt spring [Prov. 25:26].**

When I was a little boy and went along on a hunting expedition, we never carried water with us in a container. We would come to a creek or a spring. Sometimes it would be limpid water (in that day pollution was not a big problem), but every now and then we found a spring that was green with scum. What a disappointment that would be.

This is the comparison he makes with a righteous man, a man who has stood for truth, who finally bows before the wicked. How many times that happens in business. How many times that happens in politics. A man of integrity, in order to get into office, will bow before the wicked. And it even happens in the church. A man who has stood for pure doctrine, for things that are right, will begin to compromise and cut corners. That is the heartbreak of the day. It is just like coming to a spring when you are thirsty and finding it covered with scum and pollutants. What a verse this is!

> **It is not good to eat much honey: so for men to search their own glory is not glory [Prov. 25:27].**

A little honey is good, but a lot of honey makes you sick. For a man to be ambitious for self glory, especially in the ministry of God, makes you sick. We see this around us in the church—there is an inordinate ambition among some Christians today. It makes you sick at your tummy to see that type of thing.

> **He that hath no rule over his own spirit is like a city that is broken down, and without walls [Prov. 25:28].**

This refers to a man or woman who cannot control his emotions, who is not self-controlled. And you know that self-control is a fruit of the Spirit. Now there is a time for a person to let go. There is a time to stand for something and to speak out with great emotion. But, my friend, we are to recognize our need to control our own spirits.

CHAPTER 26

This first section deals with the fool. The Bible, especially Proverbs, has a great deal to say about the fool. This does not refer to the person who is mentally deficient. God is not talking to the person who is simple-minded or who has some mental aberration. The fool that God is talking to is a man who may be brilliant. In fact he may have his Ph.D. degree.

David wrote, "The fool hath said in his heart, There is no God . . ." (Ps. 14:1). A fool is a man who, though he may be brilliant, is an atheist. The Hebrew word for *fool* means "insane." The man who says there is no God is an insane man.

Intermarriage within a family can sometimes produce very brilliant offspring but can also produce mental deficiency. In the early days of a church I pastored in Tennessee one of the pastors had married into the governor's family where there had been much intermarrying. As a result, there was insanity in the family. The pastor had two daughters, and they were brilliant. They were old ladies when I was a young pastor there, living way out in the country, up in the hills of middle Tennessee. I was holding meetings in that area, and they wanted me to come by to see them. I have never met two women who were more brilliant than those ladies. They knew all about me, about the church I was serving, about the Bible, literature, music, current events. It was amazing. But there was something odd there. The pastor who went with me had warned me not to be surprised at what I would see. When we went in, we had to shoo the chickens off the chairs so we could sit down. Then we had to be rather careful where we sat. While I was sitting there talking to them, a cow stuck her head in from the kitchen door. There was a horse in the bedroom, and there were goats all around—I didn't see them, but I sure could tell they were there. The sisters had a mental aberration, you see.

Now that is not the kind of thing the Lord means when he calls a person a fool. He means someone who has rejected Him. God calls that insanity.

> **As snow in summer, and as rain in harvest, so honour is not seemly for a fool [Prov. 26:1].**

One of the marks of a fool is that he doesn't mind sacrificing his honor. Candidly, he has none.

> **As the bird by wandering, as the swallow by flying, so the curse causeless shall not come [Prov. 26:2].**

Predictions that certain things will come to pass do not always happen. By the way, we have a lot of so-called prophets in our midst today. They keep telling us what is going to happen in the next few years. Some of it may come to pass, that's true, but they are not getting their information from God—because sometimes they are wrong, and God's prophet is never wrong (see Duet. 18:20–22).

> **A whip for the horse, a bridle for the ass, and a rod for the fool's back [Prov. 26:3].**

That is a good one. The horse and the ass can be trained. They will respond. The only thing a fool will respond to is real discipline.

> **Answer not a fool according to his folly, lest thou also be like unto him.**
>
> **Answer a fool according to his folly, lest he be wise in his own conceit [Prov. 26:4–5].**

When I was a boy, our town atheist enjoyed pointing out contradictions in the Bible. This was one that he used. My friend, there is no contradiction here at all. These two proverbs simply set before us two possible lines of conduct in response to a fool.

I get many letters from many kinds of people. I answer some of the letters, and some of the letters I do not answer. I must make a decision about them. I conclude that some of the letters I get come from fools. If I were to answer such a letter according to its folly, I would make myself a fool. If you lay yourself wide open to a fool, you are a fool yourself.

I had this experience recently. I received a letter from a brilliant man who had some impressions about me that were entirely wrong. I thought I should try to correct him and tell him the truth, so I responded according to verse 5. I answered his letter. Then I received a letter back from him, and I have never seen such a foolish letter. It made me feel like a fool for having written to him in the first place. I do not intend to answer his second letter. I am using verse 4 for my decision. So you see, there are two lines of conduct set before us, and we need to determine whether we should respond or should not respond.

> **He that sendeth a message by the hand of a fool cutteth off the feet, and drinketh damage [Prov. 26:6].**

You make a mistake if you send a message by the wrong individual!

> **The legs of the lame are not equal: so is a parable in the mouth of fools [Prov. 26:7].**

I would like to extend this to the interpretation of parables. There are interpretations of parables in the Bible that are taught by some professors which tempt me to say, "So is a parable in the mouth of fools."

> **As he that bindeth a stone in a sling, so is he that giveth honour to a fool [Prov. 26:8].**

Giving honor to a fool is simply giving him ammunition.

> **As a thorn goeth up into the hand of a drunkard, so is a parable in the mouth of fools [Prov. 26:9].**

A thorny branch in the hand of a drunken man will probably wound him as well as others. The same is true of a fool who has the position of a teacher. He will hurt himself and those who listen.

The great God that formed all things both rewardeth the fool, and rewardeth transgressors [Prov. 26:10].

We can be very sure of the ultimate outcome. God will take care of things and handle all these matters.

Here is something rather frightful.

As a dog returneth to his vomit, so a fool returneth to his folly [Prov. 26:11].

I know of nothing as harsh as that. It is repulsive and sickening even to think of this. This is the viewpoint that Peter presents to us concerning the hypocrite: "But it is happened unto them according to the true proverb, The dog is turned to his own vomit again; and the sow that was washed to her wallowing in the mire" (2 Pet. 2:22).

Remember that when the prodigal son was in the pigpen, he knew that he was in the wrong place, and he returned to his home. Suppose when he returned home, he brought along with him one of the pigs from the pigpen. The little pig would not enjoy the father's house. Eventually he would go to the pigpen. Eventually, all the hypocrites in the church will be revealed, and there are many who only pretend to be sons of God—there is no question about that.

A man told me that the reason he did not join the church was that the church was filled with hypocrites. I said, "No one knows that better than I do. But that is no reason why you shouldn't be in the church. You can't hide behind a hypocrite. You should be in there revealing what is genuine."

I have talked about hypocrisy in the church before, and I receive letters from folk who don't like me to mention it. But the Bible teaches that there is a security for the believer, and also there is insecurity for the make-believer. It is to the hypocrite that the proverb refers.

> **Seest thou a man wise in his own conceit? there is more
> hope of a fool than of him [Prov. 26:12].**

There is something worse than a fool and that is an egomaniac, one
who has a high opinion of himself.

> **Where no wood is, there the fire goeth out: so where
> there is no talebearer, the strife ceaseth [Prov. 26:20].**

Bitterness is repeatedly stirred up in certain groups because there are
certain ones in there who keep putting a little wood on the fire. If no
one were fueling it, the fire would go out; the strife would cease.

> **As coals are to burning coals, and wood to fire; so is a
> contentious man to kindle strife [Prov. 26:21].**

There are certain folks who cause strife as soon as they start attending
a church or join a church. You will find them in the Lord's work today.
They seem to stir things up all the time. They are never really interested in the Word of God, although they may pretend to be.

> **The words of a talebearer are as wounds, and they go
> down into the innermost parts of the belly [Prov. 26:22].**

A better translation is, "The words of a talebearer are as dainty morsels, and go down into the innermost parts of the belly." People like to
hear those choice little bits of gossip. They like to hear them, but they
are hard to digest and will finally make them sick. A real child of God
does not wish to hear things that are ugly.

    Now here we have one of the longest and strongest sections against
hypocrisy, and it refers to hypocrisy among God's people.

> **Burning lips and a wicked heart are like a potsherd
> covered with silver dross.**

> **He that hateth dissembleth with his lips, and layeth up deceit within him;**
>
> **When he speaketh fair, believe him not: for there are seven abominations in his heart.**
>
> **Whose hatred is covered by deceit, his wickedness shall be shewed before the whole congregation.**
>
> **Whoso diggeth a pit shall fall therein: and he that rolleth a stone, it will return upon him.**
>
> **A lying tongue hateth those that are afflicted by it; and a flattering mouth worketh ruin [Prov. 26:23–28].**

There are folk who make a *profession* of faith in Jesus Christ, but who are not really God's children. We call them hypocrites because they are pretending to be what they are not. They are phonies. But they should not disturb those inside or outside the church for the very fact that a counterfeit necessitates a genuine and valuable original. No one counterfeits pennies or even one-dollar bills, as far as I know. They do counterfeit twenty-dollar bills. They only counterfeit that which is valuable. So we should not be surprised to see counterfeit Christians. This cluster of proverbs describes the phony and warns against him. He is the man who is two-faced. He will flatter you, yet in his heart he will hate you.

It was Tacitus who made the statement, "It is common for men to hate those whom they have injured." Dr. Ironside puts it like this: "Conscious of having wronged another, and being determined not to confess it, the dissembler will store his heart with hatred against the object of his wrongdoing. To hide his wretched feelings, such a one will flatter with his lips while all the time he is plotting the ruin of his victim."

An example of flattery and hypocrisy in the Bible is Haman. Remember how he flattered. This man plotted to destroy an entire people, including the queen upon the throne. He was an evil man. He flattered the king, and yet it was obvious that he was planning to overthrow the king

Hypocrisy is found in Christian circles, and we need to recognize it. There is no use covering over this. There is probably no place in the world where there is so much cover-up as in the church. We try to act as if there were no wrong there. We think that if we ignore it, it will go away. We feel defeated if anyone mentions the fact that there is hypocrisy. We feel that we in ourselves are defeated if we acknowledge that even in our hearts there is this root of bitterness sometimes. Christians need to face up to these sins, and the proverbs are good at making us face up to them.

CHAPTER 27

This chapter deals with the subject of friendship.

Boast not thyself of tomorrow; for thou knowest not what a day may bring forth [Prov. 27:1].

There is a philosophy of procrastination that is very familiar to all of us. It puts off until tomorrow what could be done today. South of the border, our Mexican friends have a word for it: "mañana"—tomorrow. That is the easy route. There is a Spanish proverb that says, "The road of by-and-by leads to the house of never." Usually when one says, *Mañana*, it really means, "Never." It is not that there is no intention of doing the thing in question. It is just put off. We have another proverb that puts it very bluntly. "The way to hell is paved with good intentions." The English have a proverb that says, "Procrastination is the thief of time." The Word of God puts it likes this: ". . . *Today* if ye will hear his voice, harden not your hearts" (Heb. 4:7, italics mine). And again, "(. . . behold, *now* is the accepted time; behold, *now* is the day of salvation.)" (2 Cor. 6:2, italics mine). Isaiah writes, "Come *now*, and let us reason together, saith the LORD . . ." (Isa. 1:18, italics mine). The tendency of man is to want to wait for another time. Remember that the governor Felix trembled when he heard the gospel from the apostle Paul. Paul, though a prisoner, talked to him about his soul's salvation, and Felix responded, ". . . Go thy way for this time; when I have a convenient season, I will call for thee" (Acts 24:25). As far as we know from the Word of God, that "convenient season" never came for Felix. Also, Pharaoh in Egypt was always going to let the children of Israel go tomorrow, not today. Finally his repeated postponements cost him his oldest son and all the firstborn in the land of Egypt.

Today is always the day of salvation. You do not know what tomorrow will bring.

Let another man praise thee, and not thine own mouth; a stranger, and not thine own lips [Prov. 27:2].

Goliath should have listened to this proverb. He paraded in front of the army of Israel every day, flexed his muscles, told them how great he was and what a miserable bunch of cowards they were. Eventually he got into trouble with a boy named David.

A stone is heavy, and the sand weighty; but a fool's wrath is heavier than them both [Prov. 27:3].

If you have a fool angry with you, you are in trouble, because a fool has no discretion. He will say and do anything.

Wrath is cruel, and anger is outrageous; but who is able to stand before envy? [Prov. 27:4].

Envy is jealousy. ". . . jealousy is cruel as the grave: the coals thereof are coals of fire, which hath a most vehement flame" (Song 8:6).

You will remember what jealousy did in the family of Jacob. The brothers sold Joseph into slavery because of their intense jealousy.

Open rebuke is better than secret love.

Faithful are the wounds of a friend; but the kisses of an enemy are deceitful [Prov. 27:5–6].

This is a contrast of which we have many examples in the Bible. Paul rebuked Simon Peter when he withdrew from eating with the Gentiles. Peter needed that rebuke, and he accepted it from Paul. There was no ill feeling between them.

It is a wonderful thing to have a friend who will call attention to your faults in a helpful way. That's the reason a preacher needs a good wife. She can keep him humble and tell him what is wrong with him. I have come out from a service puffed up like a balloon. When we get into the car, my wife pushes a pin into the balloon. I recognize that she is the one who is right rather than the one who was flattering me.

Now the contrasting thought is, of course, exemplified in Judas who betrayed Jesus with a kiss.

The full soul loatheth an honeycomb; but to the hungry soul every bitter thing is sweet [Prov. 27:7].

This is the reason we have gourmet cooking in our day. We are a pampered people who have so much to eat that the food must be prepared in unusual ways or the foods must be exotic and unusual to whet our appetites. Some people need hummingbird wings or peacock tongues served to them before they can really enjoy their food. That is why cooking reached such a high degree of perfection in the European countries like France, Italy, Spain, and Germany. The ruling class had such plenty that they got tired of eating plain food. A tenderloin steak or filet mignon or strawberries and ice cream were just not good enough for them. So the chefs of that day had to concoct unusual and tasty foods for them.

Contrast this with the hungry man. Food, all food, any food tastes good to him.

One can also apply this to the Word of God. We are to eat it, chew it, ruminate on it. Actually, this is what it means to meditate on the Word of God. May God give us an appetite, a real hunger for His Word!

As a bird that wandereth from her nest, so is a man that wandereth from his place [Prov. 27:8].

There are many folk in churches and in other Christian works who are like round pegs in square holes or square pegs in round holes. They just don't fit in. The reason is that God has given to every believer a gift: "But the manifestation of the Spirit is given to every man to profit withal" (1 Cor. 12:7, italics mine). And God has a particular place for every believer to exercise the gift he has been given: "But now hath God set the members every one of them in the body, as it hath pleased him" (1 Cor. 12:18). We should get into that place and exercise our gift. In the New Testament we have examples of folk who apparently didn't exercise their gifts. For instance, Paul spoke of a young man by the name of Demas: "For Demas hath forsaken me, having loved this present world, and is departed unto Thessalonica . . ." (2 Tim. 4:10). He went back into the world. As far as we know, he never did fit into the place that God had for him.

> **Ointment and perfume rejoice the heart: so doth the sweetness of a man's friend by hearty counsel.**
>
> **Thine own friend, and thy father's friend, forsake not; neither go into thy brother's house in the day of thy calamity: for better is a neighbour that is near than a brother far off [Prov. 27:9–10].**

I have always felt that this is a California proverb. When I first came to California, I was shocked at the few people who attended funerals. I had come from Texas, where people came from far and near to attend a · funeral. The largest crowds I ever addressed were at Texas funerals. When I came to California, I conducted a funeral for a dear saint of God who lived alone. She had brought her husband out here from the East because he was sick, and she spent much of her time caring for him until he died. She didn't have many friends although she had become active in the church to a certain extent. I thought the place would be crowded for her funeral, but there were about fifteen people there. Her family and friends were back in the East. "Better is a neighbour that is near than a brother far off." We all need friends, and it is better to make friends among our neighbors than depend on family and old friends who are great distances from us.

> **A prudent man foreseeth the evil, and hideth himself; but the simple pass on, and are punished [Prov. 27:12].**

This is one of the great benefits of the study of prophecy: We know what is coming. Frankly, I would be very discouraged and pessimistic if I had to look to men to solve our problems today. I don't think man has the solution. We are moving to a crisis and a catastrophe—I don't think there is any question about that. Any man is very foolish to think that he can solve the problems of the world. The Word of God makes it clear that there is trouble ahead, and the judgment of God is coming upon this old world.

There is another thought in connection with this proverb. I will state it in rather terse language: Buy insurance. The Lord intends for you to make plans for the future. "A prudent man foreseeth the evil, and hideth himself." He prepares for the difficult day that is coming. Some people have the idea that a man ought not prepare for retirement, ought not to carry insurance. The foolish reason given is that we ought to trust the Lord. Let me say that when the Lord has given us means for providing for the future, we should avail ourselves of them.

He that blesseth his friend with a loud voice, rising early in the morning, it shall be counted a curse to him [Prov. 27:14].

There is a great deal of irony in this statement. There are those who make such loud protestations of love and affection that you know there is some motive behind it all. Watch out for the man who is praising you more than you ought to be praised.

A scriptural illustration of this is the way in which Absalom won the hearts of the men of Israel (see 2 Sam. 15:1–6). He got up early and came to the city gate to talk to the men who came to the king with a controversy. Absalom flattered them and pretended to love them and show an interest in their cases. But his true interest was in gaining their support when he seized the throne. (Politicians have been following this same procedure from that day to this!)

I always tell this to young preachers when I am speaking in seminaries: "Young men, regardless of what church you go to, there will always be a dear saint in that church who will tell you what a wonderful preacher you are. Generally it is a sweet old lady; sometimes it is a man. The Lord puts them there to encourage young preachers. They will tell you that you are the greatest preacher they have ever heard. They will have you think you are another apostle Paul, Martin Luther, John Calvin, Billy Sunday, and Billy Graham all wrapped into one individual. It's wonderful that such a person is there to encourage you, but don't you believe what you hear. It's not true." A modern proverb goes something like this: Flattery is like perfume. The idea is to smell it, not swallow it.

Iron sharpeneth iron; so a man sharpeneth the countenance of his friend [Prov. 27:17].

It is a wonderful thing to have a friend with whom you can sharpen your mind. You can discuss certain things with him with real profit. I used to have such a friend, and we could sit down and talk about spiritual matters. I always came away refreshed and strengthened, and I always had learned something. It is wonderful to have a friend like that.

As in water face answereth to face, so the heart of man to man [Prov. 27:19]. *I think also an evil heart recognizes such & visa versa*

It is wonderful to have a friend to whom you can open your heart, knowing that he will not betray you. A friend is one who knows you and still loves you.

Hell and destruction are never full; so the eyes of man are never satisfied [Prov. 27:20].

We never see enough. We want to keep on seeing. That's the reason some of us love to travel around the world. *there is more to this proverb*

As the fining pot for silver, and the furnace for gold; so is a man to his praise [Prov. 27:21].

Be careful of praise. Make sure it has the right effect upon you. Dr. Ironside (*Notes on the Book of Proverbs*, pp. 390–391) has this comment: "There is no hotter crucible to test a man than when he is put through a fire of praise and adulation. To go on through evil report, cleaving to the Lord, and counting on Him to clear one's name is comparatively easy, though many faint in such circumstances; but to humbly pursue the even tenor of his way, undisturbed and unlifted up by applause and flattery, marks a man as being truly with God."

For riches are not for ever: and doth the crown endure to every generation? [Prov. 27:24].

"Riches are not for ever"—in our materialistic age we need to recognize the truth of this. You won't be taking your riches with you. There is no pocket in a shroud.

"And doth the crown endure to every generation?" Dynasties rise and fall in this world of changes. God is the only One on whom we can depend. He is the only unchangeable Friend.

This has been a great chapter on friendship.

CHAPTER 28

The wicked flee when no man pursueth: but the righteous are bold as a lion [Prov. 28:1].

Sin, regardless of the viewpoint of men toward it, puts a person into a state of continual fear and self-condemnation. I was speaking to a group of young people about sin, just sin in general. A young fellow and girl in the group were living together. I had never even mentioned that as a sin, but it was interesting to hear how that young man began to defend himself—it would have been amusing if it had not been so serious. When sin was being discussed, his conscience began to prick him, and then he began defending himself. "The wicked flee when no man pursueth." No one had pointed a finger at him. I would not have known of his sin if he had kept quiet. The discussion was about sin, not his particular sin.

There is a psychological term that is used: a guilt complex. We all have a guilt complex. A Christian psychologist, who was on the faculty of the University of Southern California, said to me, "We all have a guilt complex. It is as much a part of us as our right arm. No one can get rid of a guilt complex just by wishful thinking." Many people try to do that. He went on with an even more interesting statement: "We psychologists can shift the guilt complex from one place to another, but we cannot eliminate it."

"The righteous are bold as a lion." If a man is not guilty, he can stand up and speak out. If his own mind is free from guilt, he is not afraid of the thoughts and minds of other men.

He that turneth away his ear from hearing the law, even his prayer shall be abomination [Prov. 28:9].

"The Law" means the Word of God. It includes everything that had been written up to the time of Solomon: the Pentateuch, Joshua, Judges, and many of the Psalms.

The thing that God is saying here is very important. If you want God to hear you, you must hear Him first. He has made it very clear that He does not listen to the prayer of the godless man. It is just sentimental twaddle to talk about the prayers of the godless man being answered in time of trouble. Tearjerking stories tell of a sick little daughter whose father in a very sentimental way calls upon God to raise her up. I would suggest that he call a godly friend to pray to the Lord for his little girl, because God will not hear the prayer of the ungodly man. He says he won't. "For the eyes of the Lord are over the righteous, and his ears are open unto their prayers: but the face of the Lord is against them that do evil" (1 Pet. 3:12). Here in Proverbs it says that his prayer is actually an abomination to God.

> **Whoso causeth the righteous to go astray in an evil way, he shall fall himself into his own pit: but the upright shall have good things in possession [Prov. 28:10].**

This is a law of God that is operative in this world. You can find this again and again as you go through the Word of God. For example, David by his sin brought scandal into his own family and his own home.

> **The rich man is wise in his own conceit; but the poor that hath understanding searcheth him out [Prov. 28:11].**

Riches will minister to pride and conceit. They seem to go along together. You hear of rich people giving testimonies at banquets, especially prominent banquets. You hear that the great men of this world give their testimony at the president's prayer breakfast. Did you ever hear of them reaching down and asking some poor little vegetable variety Christian to give his testimony? But notice what God says,

"The rich man is wise in his own conceit; but the poor that hath understanding searcheth him out." The poor man, poor in this world's goods but rich in faith, can listen to the testimony of the rich and know that it is hollow, that it lacks reality. Even if it is real, it will often lack the ring of discernment and of understanding of spiritual things. I have been present at banquets where they have called upon a prominent businessman or a so-called Hollywood convert to give a testimony. I have noted the people who have real spiritual discernment bowing their heads in embarrassment at the things which were being said. This is a very practical proverb, and one that is often passed over.

> **He that covereth his sins shall not prosper: but whoso confesseth and forsaketh them shall have mercy [Prov. 28:13].**

This is a great proverb. It seems a common practice today for Christians to try to cover their sins. You will find in the average church that there is a Band-Aid of silence wrapped over the cancer of sin. People don't like to talk about it; in fact, they don't admit its existence. They like to think they are very good. But we are told here, "But whoso confesseth and forsaketh them shall have mercy." And we have the New Testament version of this in 1 John 1:9: "If we confess our sins, he is faithful and just to forgive us our sins, and to cleanse us from all unrighteousness." This does not refer to a public confession of sin; confession is between you and the Lord, and sin should be *dealt* with. Trying to appear sinless before your little group of friends is a big mistake. If you confess and forsake your sin, you shall have mercy. How wonderful!

> **Happy is the man that feareth alway: but he that hardeneth his heart shall fall into mischief [Prov. 28:14].**

This is what it means to walk in the fear of the Lord. Remember that "The fear of the LORD is the beginning of wisdom . . . (Prov. 9:10)." It means that our hearts are open toward God all the time. It is the opposite of "he that hardeneth his heart." The man who fears God is one who is listening to God. He is one who is trying to walk in a way that is pleasing to God. He is walking in humility before the Lord. He walks in recognition of his weakness and of his utter dependence upon God. This is the meaning of "the fear of the LORD is the beginning of wisdom."

I must pause here to say that I have received letters that read: "You have pointed out the faults of the church members, and you have given the criticism of the Christians who are in the churches today. Don't you have a word of encouragement for them?"

May I say that I attempt to teach the Word of God. We are living in days of apostasy—pastors in our churches across the land and missionaries on the foreign field are quick to acknowledge the present-day apostasy of the church. I recognize that we need encouragement, and the Bible has much to say that is encouraging to the true believer. I call attention to the local church when the Word of God makes it very clear that reference is being made to folk who are making only a profession of being Christian. I feel that to be forewarned is to be forearmed. A great many folk in and out of the church are tremendously discouraged by what they see in the lives of some Christians, and it is causing them to turn away from religion. A rebellious young man told me, "I've turned off religion." Well, knowing something of the boy's background, I almost felt like saying, I don't blame you. I couldn't say that to the young man, so I tried to point out to him that there are many wonderful saints in the church. Often they are in the background, and he hadn't noticed them. They are folk with whom he could have wonderful fellowship.

I felt that I should pause in our study to insert this explanation in case you may be thinking that I am too critical of the contemporary church.

Actually, the one who wrote these proverbs didn't spare any of us. Many of the proverbs fit us just like a garment!

A man that doeth violence to the blood of any person shall flee to the pit; let no man stay him [Prov. 28:17].

A man who is consciously guilty of having committed a horrible crime must bear a fearful load on his conscience. Often it will finally drive him to suicide. There are many cases like that today. The prime example from the Bible is Judas Iscariot who was driven to suicide because of the awful, dastardly crime which he had committed.

An FBI man told me that sometimes a crime will go unsolved for years. They will have no inkling at all of evidence nor any way to trace the guilty one. Then a man or woman pops up who has to talk, who feels impelled to make a confession. Sometimes the person is already in prison for another crime. He will confess the unsolved crime that the police are still working on. Why does he do that? Because the crime is on the mind and heart of the guilty one. There is no escape from it. God has made us that way as a means of bringing us back to Himself.

> **Whoso robbeth his father or his mother, and saith, It is no transgression; the same is the companion of a destroyer [Prov. 28:24].**

A young person may think, *I'm going to inherit what my dad owns, so I'll just take a little of it now.* God says that that is a crime. The Lord Jesus rebuked the religious rulers of His day because they taught that as soon as a person had said to his father or mother, "It is Corban" or "I have dedicated to God that which would relieve your need" (see Matt. 15:5–6; Mark 7:11), he thereby consecrated all to God and was freed from using it for his parents. This, Jesus declared to be contradictory to the command of God. You see, it is so easy because of a relationship to deny support or to take something that does not belong to us. That is what our Lord condemned.

Incidentally, if you are a parent, you should not ignore acts of theft in the home.

CHAPTER 29

He, that being often reproved hardeneth his neck, shall suddenly be destroyed, and that without remedy [Prov. 29:1].

God has so many ways of reproving a man; yet the man can keep going on in sin. In my own experience I have known so many folk who were warned before judgment fell upon them; they ignored the warning, and judgment fell upon them in this life.

In Dallas, Texas, one night I was walking down the street with a friend. A big crowd was gathered around out in front of a theatre. There was a wrecked automobile there and, believe me, it was really in a sad condition. When I got back to the seminary, one of the students told us the story of that car. It had been driven by a high school student and his girl friend. They had stopped to invite another girl to call her date and go out with them. She said, "No, I can't go with you tonight," but she asked them to come with her to a Bible class. They finally agreed to take her to her Bible class, but they would not go in with her. On the way over, this girl presented Christ to them. She told them that she had accepted Christ through the Bible class and that they needed Him, too. They just laughed, and let the girl out of the car. Five minutes later as they were speeding down the street, they were both killed instantly when they collided with another car.

There are many examples of this in the Bible. We think of Korah, and Dathan and Abiram, Belshazzar, Jezebel, and others. "He, that being often reproved hardeneth his neck, shall suddenly be destroyed, and that without remedy."

When the righteous are in authority, the people rejoice: but when the wicked beareth rule, the people mourn [Prov. 29:2].

We've seen before that when the wicked are in power, they never solve the problem, but one righteous man is able to bring blessing to a nation. That is what we need in this nation of ours above everything else. We don't need men who say they have solutions for every problem. No one has the solutions for the problems of this world, and if anyone says he does, he must say it with his tongue in his cheek. What we need today are righteous men who will stand for the right at any price. I believe just one such man is better than a whole party, regardless of what party it might be.

When the wicked rule, everyone suffers. Incidentally, for whom did you vote?

The king by judgment establisheth the land: but he that receiveth gifts overthroweth it [Prov. 29:4].

David was a good king. He was a righteous ruler over men, a ruler in the fear of God. Yet David made the confession that his house was not sound. Only Christ is the King who by judgment will establish the land. The coming of Christ to this earth is the only hope the world has. Thank the Lord that the church will leave before He comes to judge the earth. That is the promise that He has given.

Politicians today are influenced by the giving of gifts. That has always figured in the politics of both parties. The Lord Jesus will reign in *righteousness*.

A man that flattereth his neighbour spreadeth a net for his feet [Prov. 29:5].

Applause for a man who is doing a good job is certainly in order. Merit should be recognized. I think there is a time to stand up and cheer for an individual. But when flattery is used, it is like the overdose of honey that we have read about in this book. It seems there are some people who are just given to flattery. They do not really tell the thing that is upon their hearts.

When I was a pastor, there was a man who was always making requests and asking favors. I knew the minute my secretary said that he was on the phone that he wanted something. He always began the same way: "Oh Dr. McGee, I was listening to you on the radio this past week, and I want to tell you I never heard a message like that. I hope you are putting that message into print." The more flattering the things he said, the bigger the favor he was going to ask. Flattery is a dangerous thing because sometimes people believe it. It is tragic when we believe flattery.

The bloodthirsty hate the upright: but the just seek his soul [Prov. 29:10].

We might translate it like this: "Men of blood hate the perfect, but the just seek [or care] for his soul." The bloodthirsty man has murder and hate in his heart. The Lord Jesus said that if you hate your brother, you are guilty of murder.

Cain was a murderer, and the murder began in his heart. It shows how far and how quickly man fell. Remember that God created Adam and Eve *perfect*. When they fell, the only thing they could bring into the world was a sinner. They brought forth sons and daughters in their own likeness. Cain was one of them. He was a boy born with murder in his heart—he hated his brother.

A fool uttereth all his mind: but a wise man keepeth it in till afterwards [Prov. 29:11].

You talk with a fool, and he will tell you everything. A wise man will hold back. He will be very careful what he says.

If a ruler hearken to lies, all his servants are wicked [Prov. 29:12].

Parents need to discipline a child faithfully and set an example before him, because a child will imitate his parents. And the people will imitate their rulers and men in high position. The conduct of a ruler will be reflected in those who are under him. That is the picture we have here.

Correct thy son, and he shall give thee rest; yea, he shall give delight unto thy soul [Prov. 29:17].

Again we have before us the importance of discipline.

Where there is no vision, the people perish: but he that keepeth the law, happy is he [Prov. 29:18].

"Vision" is actually spiritual understanding. It is the work of the Holy Spirit in the life of the believer to give him understanding of the Word of God.

We read in 1 Samuel 3:1 ". . . And the word of the LORD was precious in those days; there was no open vision." The Word of the Lord was precious, or rare. There was no understanding of the Word of God, and therefore, it was precious in those days. God had to raise up Samuel, a seer, to meet that need.

You may remember that Joshua was disturbed because some of the men prophesied in the camp. But Moses said, ". . . would God that all the LORD'S people were prophets, and that the LORD would put his spirit upon them!" (Num. 11:29).

Spiritual discernment is one of the gifts that God has given to the church—that is, an understanding of the Word of God.

This chapter concludes the collection of proverbs that were copied out by the men of Hezekiah. It concludes all the proverbs which are attributed to King Solomon. However, I believe that the final chapter of Proverbs was also written by Solomon and that he is King Lemuel.

CHAPTER 30

In this one chapter are proverbs by an unknown sage, named Agur. The first verse tells us all we know about his parentage.

> **The words of Agur the son of Jakeh, even the prophecy: the man spake unto Ithiel, even unto Ithiel and Ucal [Prov. 30:1].**

None of these named are people whom we know. Agur is an unknown seer and unknown writer. The proper names here are like all Hebrew names in that they do mean something. *Agur* means gatherer and *Jakeh* mean pious. Some versions translate the names as common nouns: "The words of a gatherer, the son of the pious."

> **Who hath ascended up into heaven, or descended? who hath gathered the wind in his fists? who hath bound the waters in a garment? who hath established all the ends of the earth? what is his name, and what is his son's name, if thou canst tell? [Prov. 30:4].**

It is interesting to note that these are some of the questions God asked Job. Who is able to answer such questions? The Lord Jesus said, "And no man hath ascended up to heaven, but he that came down from heaven, even the Son of man which is in heaven" (John 3:13). This is why I constantly say that the Lord Jesus is the only authority on this matter of creation and the origin of the universe. Very candidly, I don't think any of us has the correct explanation of the origin of the universe. Scientists do not—the very fact that they come up with the evolutionary theory means that they do not have the answer to origin. The reason that we spent so much money to go to the moon was to get rocks so that we might find out about the origin of the universe!

The first verse of Genesis tells us that in the beginning God created the heaven and the earth. That is how it all began. But then the next verse: "And the earth was without form, and void; and darkness was upon the face of the deep. And the spirit of God moved upon the face of the waters" (Gen. 1:2) is considered by some to describe the act of creation. My friend, I don't think that God has told us *how* he did the creating. I believe this second verse suggests the gap theory—that God created the heaven and the earth and then there followed a space of time. Something happened to that original creation. The earth became without form and void. I recognize that this theory has been largely abandoned, but I still hold it in spite of what these sharp young men are writing today. My contention is that God has not told how He created. We just don't know—neither scientist nor theologian knows. I like the question God asked Job: "Where wast thou when I laid the foundations of the earth? . . ." (Job 38:4). That is a question which God can ask every individual. No one has the answer.

Also I like the question Agur asks. "Who hath gathered the wind in his fists?" Just think—God holds the winds just like we might hold some article in our hand. What a picture that is! Man knows very little about these things. In that same passage where the Lord Jesus said He was the One who came down from heaven, He also said, "The wind bloweth where it listeth, and thou hearest the sound thereof, but canst not tell whence it cometh, and whither it goeth . . ." (John 3:8). This is a tremendous thought.

> **Every word of God is pure: he is a shield unto them that put their trust in him [Prov. 30:5].**

Nothing will clean you up like the Word of God. Every Word of God is pure. It is better than any soap; it is a miracle cleanser.

> **Add thou not unto his words, lest he reprove thee, and thou be found a liar [Prov. 30:6].**

This should make us cautious in our handling of the Word of God. God doesn't mind calling a man a liar if he is one.

> **Two things have I required of thee; deny me them not before I die:**
>
> **Remove far from me vanity and lies: give me neither poverty nor riches; feed me with food convenient for me:**
>
> **Lest I be full, and deny thee, and say, Who is the LORD? or lest I be poor, and steal, and take the name of my God in vain [Prov. 30:7–9].**

"Remove far from me vanity and lies" means I don't want to live among those who are vain and are flattering and are lying. It is like living in a rattlesnake den to live with folk like that. And then he says, "Give me neither poverty nor riches." Let me take the middle of the road. I don't want to be an extremist either way.

> **There is a generation that are pure in their own eyes, and yet is not washed from their filthiness [Prov. 30:12].**

There are some church members who are like that. They are pure in their own eyes. They feel that they don't need a Savior. They are just religious.

Also there are people who are high up in business and politics who feel that they are pure—they are not guilty of wrongdoing. Even the down-and-outer may be pure in his own eyes. But none of them is washed. The only way that any of us can be clean is to be washed in the blood of Jesus Christ.

> **. . . There are three things that are never satisfied, yea, four things say not, It is enough [Prov. 30:15].**

Now he goes on to list four things that are never satisfied:

> **The grave; and the barren womb; the earth that is not filled with water; and the fire that saith not, It is enough [Prov. 30:16].**

First is "the grave." You and I live in a funeral procession. All of us do. It began outside the Garden of Eden with the death of Abel, and it has been coming down through the centuries. This old world on which we live is a great big cemetery. The grave is never satisfied.

"The barren womb." There are so many women who cannot have children for one reason or another. (I think they would make such wonderful mothers of adopted children.) They are never satisfied. Such a woman wants that precious little one to put his chubby arms around her neck and call her mother. And the same holds true for fathers.

"The earth that is not filled with water." We don't ever get enough rain out here in California. We need more rain.

"The fire that saith not, It is enough." We have too much fire and not enough rain. I sometimes wonder when we are going to burn off all the mountains of California. I thought we would have run out of burnable mountains long ago, but they still burn every summer.

The eye that mocketh at his father, and despiseth to obey his mother, the ravens of the valley shall pick it out, and the young eagles shall eat it [Prov. 30:17].

Terrible judgments are pronounced against those who turn against father and mother. God have mercy on the young people today who have turned against their parents who are believers in Christ.

There be three things which are too wonderful for me, yea, four which I know not:

The way of an eagle in the air; the way of a serpent upon a rock; the way of a ship in the midst of the sea; and the way of a man with a maid [Prov. 30:18–19].

Agur, the writer, didn't understand these things, and I don't either. Have you thought of this when you watch an eagle fly? Have you been intrigued by a serpent on a rock? Then there is the way of a ship at sea.

I went across the Atlantic on the *Queen Mary* many years ago, and it was a wonder to me how that great ship of iron could float. And then the way of a man with a maid. Today we hear so much about sex; yet in spite of that, have you noticed how awkward the young boy is when he meets a girl? They are both a little embarrassed when they meet.

I well remember my first date when I was about fourteen, before I was saved. I didn't want to miss anything so I started to date early. I was walking with this girl, taking her to a movie. In those days men wore garters to hold up their socks. Well, mine came loose, and it was dragging. Oh my! You talk about embarrassment! I never was so embarrassed in all my life. I didn't have sense enough to just stop and step aside to fix it. I just went down the street dragging that garter. After a while a crowd followed us, and that made it even worse. The girl got red in the face, and I got red in the face. I don't think we said anything to each other for a couple of hours after that happened. The way of a man with a maid. Agur says that he doesn't understand these things, and I don't understand them either.

Such is the way of an adulterous woman; she eateth, and wipeth her mouth, and saith, I have done no wickedness [Prov. 30:20].

We are living in a day when this has come to pass. There are those who are living in sin, and they will argue that they are not living in sin. I understand one little girl born out of wedlock was given a name that means purity. Well, in the first place the child was not pure because *all* children are born with a sinful nature. In the second place, the name of the child would not change the fact that her mother was an adulteress. God says that adultery is sin, and God has not changed His mind. He hasn't learned anything new from this generation. God knew the sins that our generation would commit, and He has already written about them in the Book of Proverbs.

For three things the earth is disquieted, and for four which it cannot bear:

**For a servant when he reigneth; and a fool when he is
filled with meat [Prov. 30:21–22].**

"For a servant when he reigneth"—that was Jeroboam who was a servant and became the first king of the northern kingdom of Israel.

Then "a fool when he is filled with meat" is typified by the rich fool our Lord told about who built bigger barns. With financial success like that, he was eating gourmet food, of course. He was a fool and he was "filled with meat."

The third thing is—

**For an odious woman when she is married; and an
handmaid that is heir to her mistress [Prov. 30:23].**

"For an odious woman when she is married" doesn't require a comment—I think we all get the picture.

"And an handmaid that is heir to her mistress." Sometimes a very poor person, who has been walked on, suddenly becomes rich. There is no one who is more overbearing than such a person.

Now we are going to visit a zoo to look at some of the animals there. Did you know that animals have a message for us? God created them for His many purposes. One of those purposes is to give a message to us.

**There be four things which are little upon the earth, but
they are exceeding wise [Prov. 30:24].**

God says we can learn from the animal world. The first group is made up of small creatures, little bitty animals. In fact, the first is an insect, the ant.

**The ants are a people not strong, yet they prepare their
meat in the summer [Prov. 30:25].**

Now we are going to find two groups of animals listed here. The first group is an illustration of the way to God for the sinner. The second group is an illustration of the walk of the saints before God.

Those little creatures, the ants, are wise, and we can learn from them. We have already seen in Proverbs 6:6–8: "Go to the ant, thou sluggard; consider her ways, and be wise; which having no guide, overseer, or ruler, provideth her meat in the summer, and gathereth her food in the harvest." Ants do gather grain. I have seen them do it in Texas and in Palestine. A little ant will carry a grain of wheat or oats that is bigger than the ant. They store up food during those brief and bright days of harvest. The ant is an example to us of wisdom in preparing for the future with material things.

Some people think that Christians should not have insurance but they ought to trust the Lord for their future. Friend, I think we should have everything that is available to us. If the Lord has given us means of caring for our future, we should have insurance and a savings account and a home, if it is possible. We should make a will to provide for the future of our loved ones. That is what the ant teaches us. He takes out insurance for his future by storing his food in the time of harvest.

There is a deeper message here. There are so many people who make no arrangement beyond death. They may go to the undertaker and arrange for their funeral. I saw the advertisement of an undertaker which read: "Lay away plan: pay now and go later." That is not the kind of arrangement beyond death that I mean. I am speaking of eternity. We are here for a few fleeting moments of time, and then there will be the endless ages of eternity. Isn't it foolish to care for the physical body and neglect the soul? Isn't it foolish to make no preparation for eternity?

The wicked emperor of Rome, Hadrian, said something like this when he was dying: "No more crown for this head, no more beauty for these eyes, no more music for these ears, and no more food for this stomach of mine. But my soul, oh, my soul, what is to become of you?" It is a certainty that we shall die. "And as it is appointed unto men once to die, but after this the judgment" (Heb. 9:27). It is possible to live for this life only, to eat, drink, and be merry, for tomorrow we die. A person can spend his time building bigger barns, but God tells us to be prepared to meet our God.

The conies are but a feeble folk, yet make they their houses in the rocks [Prov. 30:26].

Now the conies are the next animal we visit. The "conies" are not to be confused with the conies of England, which are actually rabbits. These "conies" are the *hyrax syriacus*. They have long hair, a short tail, and round ears. They are "feeble" and defenseless. They are not able to burrow in the ground, which makes them vulnerable little creatures; so they hide in the rocks to find a place of safety. They are included in the Leviticus list of unclean animals.

The coney has a message for man. Like the coney, man is poor, helpless, and unclean. We are sinners, and we need to recognize our pitiful plight. This is why David prays, ". . . Lead me to the rock that is higher than I" (Ps. 61:2). We sing this in the hymn "The Rock That is Higher Than I" by E. Johnson:

> Oh, then to the Rock let me fly,
> To the Rock that is higher than I.

That Rock is none other than the Lord Jesus Christ.

The locusts have no king, yet go they forth all of them by bands [Prov. 30:27].

The locust is a creature of destruction. Joel had a great deal to say about the locust plagues. We find locusts again in the Book of Revelation. They devour all the leaves and the vegetation. On one of my visits to Palestine, they were not having a real plague of them, but there were quite a few locusts, especially around the Sea of Galilee. They were doing a good job of destroying everything in their way. They are creatures of destruction.

"The locusts have no king." They have no visible head or leader, yet they go forth like soldiers in their respective regiments. They move so methodically that they seem to be acting under definite instructions and strict discipline.

To us as believers they furnish an example of subjection to one another and subjection to our unseen Head in heaven. To the world the body of believers must look like disorganized, fragmented, unrelated groups of people, with no leader and no bond of union. But, my friend, we do have a Leader. Christ is the unseen Head of the church. The apostle Paul wrote to the Corinthian believers: "For ye are yet carnal: for whereas there is among you envying, and strife, and divisions, are ye not carnal, and walk as men?" (1 Cor. 3:3). Not only is Christ the Head of all who have been redeemed by the blood of Christ, but the Holy Spirit is indwelling every believer, welding us together in one great family, ". . . every one members one of another" (Rom. 12:5). This is what the locust is teaching us.

The spider taketh hold with her hands, and is in kings' palaces [Prov. 30:28].

The Hebrew word for "spider" is *shemameth* and refers to a little house lizard. Delitzsch says, "The lizard thou canst catch with the hand and yet it is in kings' palaces." Somehow or other it can work its way into houses, and it has an affinity for fine tapestry and palatial mansions. It has fanlike feet which exude a sticky substance so that the lizard can actually hold onto a marble wall or a tessellated ceiling.

This teaches us about faith, the kind of faith that takes hold of the promises of God. It is the faith that enters into the very heavenly places. It lays hold of the fact that the Spirit of God Himself beareth witness with our spirit, that we are the sons of God. It is the faith that says, ". . . I know whom I have believed, and am persuaded that he is able to keep that which I have committed unto him against that day" (2 Tim. 1:12). "Being confident of this very thing, that he which hath begun a good work in you will perform it until the day of Jesus Christ" (Phil. 1:6).

Now we come to the second group.

There be three things which go well, yea, four are comely in going:

A lion which is strongest among beasts, and turneth not away for any [Prov. 30:29–30].

The lion goes straight ahead and doesn't detour. He is not afraid of the pussycats in the neighborhood—they don't frighten him. A lion is known for its unflinching boldness, and this should characterize the Christian as we earnestly contend for the faith. I think of the apostle Paul who in the face of suffering and persecution said, "But none of these things move me, neither count I my life dear unto myself, so that I might finish my course with joy, and the ministry, which I have received of the Lord Jesus, to testify the gospel of the grace of God" (Acts 20:24).

I think that the curse of the church today lies in pussyfooting preachers and mealymouthed deacons.

It is said of Cromwell that he was a man without fear. When asked why, he said, "I have learned that when you fear God you have no man to fear."

General "Stonewall" Jackson, a Christian man, got his appellation because one day in battle the men of General Cox were ready to retreat. General Cox looked over at him and then said to his men, "Look at General Jackson; he's standing like a stone wall." He was a man of course, like a lion. That is the way the walk of the believer should be.

The next animal is a greyhound.

A greyhound; an he goat also; and a king, against whom there is no rising up [Prov. 30:31].

The greyhound we are speaking of here is not the Greyhound Bus! The Christian is to be like a greyhound in that he is to gird up his loins and run with patience the race that is set before him. "Wherefore seeing we also are compassed about with so great a cloud of witnesses, let us lay aside every weight, and the sin which doth so easily beset us, and let us run with patience the race that is set before us, looking unto Jesus the author and finisher of our faith . . ." (Heb. 12:1–2).

The other animal mentioned in this verse is the goat. The mountain goat is a climber who lives way up in the top of the mountains. He finds both pleasure and safety in his high retreat.

The lesson is plain to see. The believer who walks on the high places, as did Habakkuk, will be able to rejoice in the day of trouble. "Although the fig tree shall not blossom, neither shall fruit be in the vines; the labour of the olive shall fail, and the fields shall yield no meat; the flock shall be cut off from the fold, and there shall be no herd in the stalls: yet I will rejoice in the LORD, I will joy in the God of my salvation. The LORD God is my strength, and he will make my feet like hinds' feet, and he will make me to walk upon mine high places . . ." (Hab. 3:17–19).

CHAPTER 31

The final chapter of Proverbs is designated as the words of King Lemuel. A popular title would be, "Advice on how to choose a wife."

> **The words of king Lemuel, the prophecy that his mother taught him [Prov. 31:1].**

I believe this chapter was written by Solomon. There is no king named Lemuel. The name that God gave to Solomon is *Jedidiah*, which means "beloved of the Lord" (2 Sam. 12:25); the name *Lemuel* means "devoted to the Lord." My guess is that this was the pet name that Bathsheba had for Solomon.

I have a notion that every man reading this can remember a pet name that his mother had for him. You would almost be ashamed to say what it was, wouldn't you? Probably Solomon's mother had a pet name for him, and I think it was Lemuel. Around the palace you probably could have heard her calling, "Lemuel."

This was a mother's advice to her son. It makes a great Mother's Day sermon, by the way.

> **What, my son? and what, the son of my womb? and what, the son of my vows? [Prov. 31:2].**

Bathsheba is asking, "What can I say to you?" She needed to say something, because she saw in this boy Solomon some of the characteristics of his father David. She well remembered the sin of David. I don't think it was her sin; I think it was David's sin. In the first chapter of Matthew it says, ". . . and David the king begat Solomon of her that had been the wife of Urias" (Matt. 1:6). Bathsheba's name is not even mentioned. I believe God is making it clear that it was David's sin. She sees the temptation that Solomon faces; so she gives him words of advice. "What, my son? What can I say to you, son of my womb? You're my precious boy, the son of my vows"—she had dedicated him to God.

> **Give not thy strength unto women, nor thy ways to that which destroyeth kings [Prov. 31:3].**

She knew David.

> **It is not for kings, O Lemuel, it is not for kings to drink wine; nor for princes strong drink:**
>
> **Lest they drink, and forget the law, and pervert the judgment of any of the afflicted [Prov. 31:4–5].**

We are told that every day in Washington there are many cocktail parties for our government officials. Republicans and Democrats both have this in common—the party membership doesn't make any difference. It is tragic to have drinking men in high positions of government!

> **Give strong drink unto him that is ready to perish, and wine unto those that be of heavy hearts.**
>
> **Let him drink, and forget his poverty, and remember his misery no more [Prov. 31:6–7].**

She tells Solomon to use wine for medicine.

> **Open thy mouth for the dumb in the cause of all such as are appointed to destruction.**
>
> **Open thy mouth, judge righteously, and plead the cause of the poor and needy [Prov. 31:8–9].**

Oh, Solomon, be honest and just and fair!

Now she goes on to tell him how to choose a wife. This is good advice. It is God's advice.

Who can find a virtuous woman? for her price is far above rubies [Prov. 31:10].

"Virtuous" here means a woman of character, a woman of strength, a woman of real ability. She is not to be a shrinking violet. She is not to be like Whistler's mother, always sitting in a rocking chair. (A whimsical story is told that Whistler painted another picture of his mother, because he came in one day and found her sitting on the floor and said to her, "Mother, you're off your rocker.") I don't think you will find many mothers sitting in rocking chairs. They are busy. This is the picture of a busy mother:

The heart of her husband doth safely trust in her, so that he shall have no need of spoil [Prov. 31:11].

She will be faithful. "He shall have no need of spoil." She will not be a spendthrift with her husband's money. She will be a helpmate or a helpmeet for him. God never intended woman to be a servant of man. She is to be his partner, and a real partner. When God made Eve to be a helpmeet, He made the other half of Adam. Adam was only half a man until God made Eve and gave her to him.

She will do him good and not evil all the days of her life [Prov. 31:12].

She is a real helpmeet.

She seeketh wool, and flax, and worketh willingly with her hands [Prov. 31:13].

She doesn't mind working.

She is like the merchants' ships; she bringeth her food from afar [Prov. 31:14].

She looks for bargains to spend the money wisely.

She riseth also while it is yet night, and giveth meat to her household, and a portion to her maidens [Prov. 31:15].

She knows how to keep a house. She runs a night shift and is a wonderful mother.

I do not recall any time when I was growing up as a boy that I got up in the morning and found my mother in bed. I just thought about that the other day. Later on when she became old, it was different, of course. But when I was a boy, by the time I got out of bed, she was up, and breakfast was usually ready and on the table.

She considereth a field, and buyeth it: with the fruit of her hands she planteth a vineyard.

She girdeth her loins with strength, and strengtheneth her arms [Prov. 31:16–17].

She is a woman of ability. She runs her household well.

She perceiveth that her merchandise is good: her candle goeth not out by night [Prov. 31:18].

She proves the adage, "Man's work is from sun to sun, but a woman's work is never done."

She layeth her hands to the spindle, and her hands hold the distaff.

She stretcheth out her hand to the poor; yea, she reacheth forth her hands to the needy [Prov. 31:19–20].

She is a generous person.

> **She is not afraid of the snow for her household: for all
> her household are clothed with scarlet [Prov. 31:21].**

I was remembering that my mother kept my pants patched when I was
a boy.

> **She openeth her mouth with wisdom; and in her tongue
> is the law of kindness [Prov. 31:26].**

She is both wise and kind in her advice and admonitions.

> **Favour is deceitful, and beauty is vain: but a woman
> that feareth the LORD, she shall be praised [Prov. 31:30].**

Young man, first you should look for a wife who is a Christian. Then I
hope that you get a good-looking one in the bargain—it's nice to have
both together. "A woman that feareth the LORD, she shall be praised."
This is of prime importance.

> **Give her of the fruit of her hands; and let her own works
> praise her in the gates [Prov. 31:31].**

I guess this is the reason we have Mother's Day, a day to honor our
mothers. However, there are many mothers who are not worthy of the
tribute given to mothers on Mother's Day.

This Book of Proverbs has been a book for young men. Also it is a
wonderful book for young ladies. In fact, we all can learn from the
wisdom in this remarkable book.

BIBLIOGRAPHY
(Recommended for Further Study)

Arnot, William. *Laws from Heaven for Life on Earth*. London, England: T. Nelson and Sons, 1864.

Bridges, Charles. *An Exposition of Proverbs*. Carlisle, Pennsylvania: The Banner of Truth Trust, 1959.

Darby, J. N. *Synopsis of the Books of the Bible*. Oak Park, Illinois: Bible Truth Publishers, n.d.

Gaebelein, Arno C. *The Annotated Bible*. Neptune, New Jersey: Loizeaux Brothers, 1917.

Gray, James M. *Synthetic Bible Studies*. Old Tappan, New Jersey: Fleming H. Revell Co., 1906.

Ironside, H. A. *Notes on the Book of Proverbs*. Neptune, New Jersey: Loizeaux Brothers, 1907. (Very good.)

Jensen, Irving L. *Proverbs*. Chicago, Illinois: Moody Press, 1982.

Kelly, William. *The Proverbs*. Oak Park, Illinois: Bible Truth Publishers, n.d.

Kidner, D. *The Proverbs*. Chicago, Illinois: InterVarsity Christian Fellowship, 1964.

Mackintosh, C. H. *Miscellaneous Writings*. Neptune, New Jersey: Loizeaux Brothers, n.d.

Moorehead, W. G. *Outline Studies in the Old Testament*. Grand Rapids, Michigan: Zondervan Publishing House, 1894.

Sauer, Erich. *The Dawn of World Redemption*. Grand Rapids, Michigan: William B. Eerdmans Publishing Co., 1951. (An excellent Old Testament survey.)

Scroggie, W. Graham. *The Unfolding Drama of Redemption.* Grand Rapids, Michigan: Zondervan Publishing House, 1970. (An excellent survey and outline of the Old Testament.)

Unger, Merrill F. *Unger's Bible Handbook.* Chicago, Illinois: Moody Press, 1966.

Unger, Merrill F. *Unger's Commentary on the Old Testament.* Vol. 1. Chicago, Illinois: Moody Press, 1981. (A fine summary of each chapter.)